THE DEVELOPMENT OF THE ORGANISATION
OF ANGLO-AMERICAN TRADE
1800-1850

THE

DEVELOPMENT OF THE ORGANISATION

OF

ANGLO-AMERICAN TRADE

1800-1850

BY

NORMAN SYDNEY BUCK, Ph.D.

ARCHON BOOKS
1969

SBN: 208 00746 6
Library of Congress Catalog Card Number: 69-13626
Printed in the United States of America

PREFACE

THIS monograph is offered to those students of economic history who believe, with the writer, that one of the needs of the present time is a better understanding of the origin of our business organisation, its forms and its functions. Perhaps more questions and problems will have been raised than have been definitely settled, but it seems to the writer that far too little attention has in the past been paid to the period under discussion, and that he will have rendered a service if he succeeds only in stimulating further research and investigation.

The writer would acknowledge his great obligation to Professors Clive Day and Edgar S. Furniss of Yale University, who have been unfailing in their interest and particularly helpful in reading and criticising the entire manuscript.

NORMAN SYDNEY BUCK.

New Haven, Connecticut,
June, 1924.

CONTENTS

CONTENTS

CHAPTER I

INTRODUCTION

THE general purpose of this study is to investigate the methods of buying and selling goods entering into the trade between the United States and Great Britain at the opening of the nineteenth century, and to trace the developments and modifications in these methods through the period from 1800 to 1850. In order to make the study as concrete as possible, especial attention will be paid to the marketing of American raw cotton, and of British manufactured goods.

In the discussion of the organisation it has been found necessary to ignore such topics as insurance, transportation, communication, and commercial policy, and to focus the attention upon the more important of the agencies directly engaged in the buying and selling, or in the financing of goods destined for the foreign market. More specifically, it is a study of the operations of the importing and exporting merchant and commission merchant, the broker, and the financial houses which aided in the carrying on of foreign commerce through the extension of credit.

The period from 1800 to 1850 seems peculiarly appropriate for study. The trade between Great Britain and America was then of real significance, large enough in volume to admit of the establishment of settled business customs. From the standpoint of the United States, Great Britain was the most important country with which it had trade relations. The following table, which gives for certain years the value of the commerce of the United States with Great Britain, as compared with the total foreign commerce of the United States, illustrates very clearly the importance of the British market to the American merchants and consumers.

Total Value of Merchandise imported from and exported to the United Kingdom and all other countries, respectively, in the Foreign Trade of the United States, with the Percentages of Total Values from and to the United Kingdom during each Period of Five Years, from 1821 to 1850.[1]

Periods of Five Years	Imports from United Kingdom	All other countries	Percentage from United Kingdom
1821-25	$151,346,561	$217,885,821	40.39%
1826-30	138,667,139	221,589,264	38.77
1831-35	219,976,517	317,452,362	40.93
1836-40	254,414,559	403,363,348	38.68
1841-45	178,359,348	298,895,659	37.37
1846-50	285,730,187	417,962,596	40.60

Periods of Five Years	Exports to United Kingdom	All other countries	Percentage to United Kingdom
1821-25	$122,154,837	$221,828,068	35.51%
1826-30	117,569,294	232,758,038	33.56
1831-35	188,287,249	270,533,755	41.04
1836-40	273,849,766	302,831,240	47.49
1841-45	221,175,606	285,131,492	43.68
1846-50	349,495,899	339,746,360	50.71

The trade with America was perhaps not so important from the British point of view, yet the table which follows indicates that the exports and imports to and from the United States did not form an inconsiderable part of the total foreign trade of Great Britain.

Real or Declared Value of British and Irish Produce and Manufactures Exported.

Year	Total Exported[2]	Exported from the United Kingdom to the United States[3]
1805	£38,077,144	£11,011,409
1810	48.438,680	10,920,752
1815	51,503,028	13,255,374
1820	36,424,652	3,875,286
1825	38,877,388	7,018,934
1830	38,271,597	6,132,346
1835	47,372,270	10,568,455
1840	51,406,430	5,283,020
1845	60,111,081	7,142,839
1849	63,596,025	11,971,028

[1] Statistical Tables, H. R. Mis. Doc. No. 117, 52d Cong., 2d Sess., 1893, pp. x-xi. Satisfactory statistics showing the imports from the United Kingdom have not been discovered for the years before 1820, but the figures given above serve to illustrate the point in question.

[2] Porter, G. R., *The Progress of the Nation* (revised ed. by F. W. Hirst), 1912, p. 477.

[3] *Ibid.*, pp. 479, 480.

Official Value of Imports into Great Britain.

Year	Foreign and Colonial Imports[4]	Imports from the United States[5]
1801	£31,786,262	£ 2,706,518
1805	28,561,270	1,766,556
1810	39,301,612	2,614,405
1815	32,987,396	2,370,288
1820	32,438,650	3,651,342
1825	44,137,482	5,716,252
1830	46,245,241	8,055,962
1835	48,911,542	10,357,743
1840	67,432,964	18,062,638

It is not, however, the value of the exchanges between the two countries which makes the trade of this period so significant, but rather the fact that the volume of trade was increasing, and, in particular, that the quantity of certain articles of commerce exchanged—notably raw cotton and cotton textiles—increased at a very rapid rate.[6]

This expansion of trade, resulting from the revolutionary changes in the technique of production, in transportation, and in banking, which made it possible for the producer to supply distant markets with a larger quantity of goods at a lower price than formerly, makes the period an extremely important one for the study of the effects of economic changes on business organisation. As a consequence of the increased volume of goods to be handled we should expect to find the foreign trade organisation adapting itself to the new conditions, and to discover certain forms of business, or methods of buying and selling goods, showing themselves incapable of coping with the situation, and new forms and methods springing up, more suited to the new order of things.

[4] Porter, G. R., *Progress of the Nation* (revised ed. by F. W. Hirst), 1912, p. 477.

[5] MacGregor, *Commercial Statistics*, 1850, vol. III, p. 800. These figures, which represent quantities and not values, obviously cannot be taken as giving a complete picture of the trade relations, but they give a basis for a rough comparison, sufficient for our purposes.

[6] *Cf.* Chapter III, pp. 31-36, for statistics of cotton exports. *Cf.* Chapter VII, p. 166, for statistics of exports of cotton goods.

CHAPTER II

THE AGENCIES OF TRADE

It is not within the scope of this chapter to treat in detail of the nature and operations of all the different business units which assisted in the handling of the goods entering into the foreign trade between Great Britain and the United States. Our intention is rather to give a brief sketch of certain of the forms of organisation obtaining in the period from 1800 to 1850, to serve as an introduction to the more intensive study of the marketing of raw cotton and of the manufactured goods of Great Britain. From this standpoint the nature of the operations and the commercial position of the merchant, the commission merchant or factor, and the broker will be considered briefly, ignoring the agents connected with the financing, insuring, and transporting of the goods.

Our discussion will be devoted chiefly to the British merchant, factor, and broker, not because the American merchants and factors are considered to be less important, but partially because the material necessary to make a fairly complete picture is more abundant for the British agents of trade; and partially because it has been felt that a description of both the British merchant and the American merchant, so far as either was engaged in the Anglo-American commerce, would be a needless duplication. Obviously the American merchant and the British merchant had in a large measure the same background; they operated under laws which were very similar, and, in consequence, each pursued methods which were almost identical.

THE MERCHANT

The term "merchant" had a very definite connotation to writers on commerce, but the use of the term in everyday speech or writings was quite vague and elusive. Montefiore defined a merchant as a person who bought and sold commodities in wholesale quantities, or who traded commercially by exporting or importing on his own account. This definition excludes retailers, agents, factors, and brokers of every description. It also excludes what he called "warehouse men"—"those who transact business by keeping goods ready in their possession."

"Merchants, properly so-called," he continued, "are of two descriptions, such as general merchants, who deal to all parts, and indiscriminately in every article in gross, and such as deal only in one article, or with one country. Thus there are West India merchants, Russia, Turkey, Spanish, and American merchants. . . ."[1]

The looseness in the use of the term makes it particularly difficult to form an accurate notion of the importance of this class which traded on its own account. A witness, called upon to testify before a Parliamentary Committee, might state that he was a merchant, but the description of his business which followed would indicate quite unmistakably that he was a commission merchant, acting as an agent for others. There were, of course, merchants in the true sense of the word. Thomas Oldham was a merchant dealing chiefly in linens, and he himself stated that he bought and sold on his own account entirely, and took no consignments in any way.[2] George Ranking was another early British merchant, dealing in Irish and German linens, who, so far as one can judge from his testimony, could not be considered a factor.[3] Walter Fergus, a Scottish manufacturer of linens, sold his goods to merchants of Glasgow, Liverpool, and London. These were merchants, trading with America only, and buying goods outright.[4]

Among the Americans were to be found many individuals who were properly called merchants, but probably the greater part

---

[1] Montefiore, *Commercial Dict.*, 1803, (no paging) art. Merchants.

The following testimony supports Montefiore's general classification:

"Do the merchants you speak of, reside at Glasgow? Glasgow, chiefly, and Liverpool and London.

"Do you know that they do not trade to the West Indies as well as to America? I know the merchants I allude to, do no trading to the West Indies; there is some export to the West Indies.

"Of the linens made in your district? Yes.

"Are they not also sent by the same houses? Not the same houses I allude to; they are sent by the West India houses, but the trade in general is distinct." Parl. Papers, Orders in Council, 1812 (210), p. 477.

[2] Parl. Papers, Report on Linen Trade, 1822, VII (560), p. 96.

[3] Parl. Papers, Report on Foreign Trade, 1820, II (300), p. 73.

[4] Parl. Papers, Orders in Council, 1812, p. 477.

were engaged in trade to the Far East, and not in the Anglo-American trade, although in the second quarter of the century a fairly numerous and important group of merchant importers arose.

Many of the British mercantile houses bought goods outright; in a later chapter it will be shown that the common method of handling the British manufactured goods before 1815 was by purchases by the merchants. But most of these houses also received goods on consignment from the manufacturers, and from the planters or merchants in America.[5]

The merchant who both bought and sold on his own account, and who never acted as a factor, seems to have been a much less significant figure than the commission merchant in the foreign trade of the period.[6]

THE COMMISSION MERCHANT OR FACTOR

The attempt is sometimes made to distinguish between a factor and a commission merchant, but so far as we can see, there is no practical difference between the two terms. In fact, a commission merchant is a factor.[7] Possibly there are certain differences in the ideas suggested by the two words, for while the term "factor" always denotes an agent of a particular sort, the word "commission merchant" in any specific case is much more vague and undefinable. Partners who described themselves as commission merchants were factors, but in actuality they might have been much more than factors. In this section, however, and throughout this study we shall consider the two terms as synonymous.

DEFINITION OF A FACTOR

A factor may be defined as an agent empowered by an individual or individuals to transact business on his or their account. Usually he was not resident in the same place as his principal, but in a foreign country, or at a distance. The busi-

---

5 *Vide* Chapter V.

6 *Vide* pp. 10 ff.

7 "A commission merchant is a factor to whom goods are usually consigned for sale, by merchants residing abroad or at a distance from the place of sale. But his rights and duties are neither increased nor diminished by the mode in which the goods are delivered to him, nor by the residence of his principal, where he resides in the same country." Edwards, *Brokers and Factors*, 1870, p. 26.

ness which he transacted depended on the authority given him
by his principal, and might be limited to a particular and
specific transaction, or might be more extended, and comprise
buying and selling, shipping, negotiating insurance, discounting
bills, making payments, etc. He could, and in many cases did, do
anything which the principal himself could do through an agent.
A distinctive mark of the factor seems to have been that he was
permitted to transact business in his own name and as if on his
own account.[8]

The relations of the principal and his factor were governed by
the general laws of agency. The principal was bound by the
acts of his factor in so far as he had given him authority to act,
or so far as general mercantile custom would sanction the acts
of a factor which were incidental to the performance of the particular item of business for the employer. It was stated, for example, that the law in America did not allow a factor to give
credit for articles which he sold, but that if express permission
to sell on credit had been given, or a general mercantile custom
of giving credit were found to prevail, a loss arising from the
failure of the vendee would fall upon the principal.[9] This rule
held also in England, where the agent or factor with *general*
orders to sell was bound to use "that diligence a prudent man

[8] "A factor is a commercial agent, transacting the mercantile affairs of
other men, in consideration of a fixed salary, and on certain commission."
Caines, *Lex. Merc. Am.*, 1802, p. 388.

"An agent, sometimes called Factor, is the representative of his employer, and in most cases, particularly in the foreign trade, the business he
transacts is conducted in his own name, and as upon his own account."
Tate, *Elements*, 1819, I, p. 116.

"FACTOR, an agent employed by some one individual or individuals, to
transact business on his or their account. He is not generally resident in
the same place as his principal, but usually in a foreign country. He is
authorised, either by letter of attorney or otherwise, to receive, buy and
sell goods and merchandise; and, generally to transact all sorts of business on account of his employers, under such limitations and conditions as
the latter may choose to impose." McCulloch, *Dictionary*, 1834, p. 568.

[9] "The strict rule of law is that factors cannot give credit for the
articles which they sell: and if they do, it is at their own peril: this maxim
is founded on the principle before noticed, that payment is by our juris-
prudence due on delivery, unless the contrary be agreed. . . .

"But in a deviation from this, either express permission, or the usage
of custom will excuse; in either of these cases, the loss arising from the
failure of a vendee, must be borne by the principal; . . .

"In the State of New York, and generally throughout the Union the
usage of trade warrants the factor in giving credit at the risk of his

would use in his own affairs." He might sell on credit if the general custom of the trade was to sell on credit, and the vendee were a person of good repute. But if the principal had stipulated that the goods were to be sold for cash and at a certain price, he had no right to deviate from those terms, and was held liable if he did so. When he sold on credit, the terms had to be reasonable and the security such as the principal might avail himself of by "reasonable diligence, and without any extraordinary risk or trouble."[10]

TYPES OF COMMISSION HOUSES

The general Commission House. Commission houses were of several different types. There was, of course, the general commission house which handled any article of commerce, and exported and imported to and from every port. The firm of Ewart, Meyers and Company, of London and Liverpool, offered an example of such a commission house. It was engaged in buying and selling on commission the produce and wares of England, the Continent, the United States, the West Indies, the East Indies, and South America.[11] The firm of Thomas Wilson and Company did a similar sort of business. It received consignments of silk from Italy, of wool from Germany, of cotton from the United States, and exported manufactured goods to the United States.[12] S. Friday and Bourcard were general agents purchasing on commission all kinds of West India and East India produce, and receiving consignments,[13] and many similar examples might be given.

Commission Houses Trading to One Market. We find, however, a certain degree of specialisation among commission merchants, similar to that which we found in the case of merchants. Certain houses dealt solely or principally with a certain market. Thus there were American, Russian, Brazilian, Indian, and con-

principal when the contrary is not stipulated or enjoined." Caines, *Lex. Merc. Am.*, 1802, p. 491.

"Thus a factor may sell goods upon credit, that being in the ordinary course of conducting mercantile affairs; . . ." McCulloch, *Dictionary*, 1834, p. 588.

[10] Chitty, *Treatise*, 1824, III, p. 218.
[11] Parl. Papers, Report on Manufactures, 1833, p. 246.
[12] *Ibid.*, p. 91.
[13] Parl. Papers, Report on Grain, 1814-1815, V (26), p. 46.

tinental commission merchants. William Higgins, of London, stated that he dealt with Malta only, and with no other part of the Mediterranean.[14] The house of Baring Brothers and Company exported woolens, cottons, hardware, etc., and received consignments of cotton and other produce. They did deal with more than one market, but their principal trade was with America. In other words, they were American Commission Merchants.[15] Charles Ogleby was a continental merchant; he received goods from the Continent for sale in Great Britain, and bought goods there on commission to ship to the Continent.[16] Freeze maintained a house in London and one in Rio Janeiro for the handling of his South American trade; he received in South America consignments of every description of woolen, linen, and cotton manufacture, and "almost every article of commerce," and from South America consigned produce to the London house.[17] Lancaster was another merchant principally engaged in the Brazil trade, exporting linens from Great Britain and importing the produce of Brazil.[18] Charles Lyne, of London, was asked in 1812 if there were not houses dealing solely with Brazil, and replied that many houses of business had been established in London and Liverpool with a view solely to the Brazil trade.[19] There were likewise India merchants. Patrick M'Lachlan described himself as a merchant and agent to India, exporting British goods to India, apparently partly on commission and partly on his own account.[20]

Commission Houses Trading in One Article. There was another form of specialisation, aside from this concentration on a particular market, and that was with respect to goods. One merchant was principally interested in the export of linens, or woolens, or hardware, or he might be engaged solely in the import of cotton from the United States, or from the West Indian islands, or of wool from Spain.

In 1795 Everitt, a factor of London, asserted that his business was principally the export of woolens to Ireland and the

14 Parl. Papers, Orders in Council, 1812, p. 663.
15 Parl. Papers, Report on Manufactures, 1833, pp. 45-47.
16 Parl. Papers, Report on Merchants, 1823, p. 90.
17 Parl. Papers, Report on Foreign Trade, 1820, II (300), p. 115.
18 *Ibid.,* p. 91.
19 Parl. Papers, Orders in Council, 1812, p. 645.
20 Parl. Papers, Report on Foreign Trade, 1821, VI (746), p. 277.

foreign countries.[21] William Tate was even more explicit in stating the nature of his business; he said, "My trade lies only in cottons and linens of all denominations."[22]

Few of the corn factors seem to have been engaged in any other line of business. Our evidence is largely inferential, but in the various reports dealing with different phases of the corn trade, the only corn factors noted as dealing in other articles than corn were two general commission firms which appear to have imported corn on occasion.[23]

The determination of the relative importance of these different types of commission houses seems to be quite impossible. Possibly with a growth in the volume of exports and imports we should expect to find a greater degree of specialisation among the different houses; and this seems to have been true in the case of the trade in raw cotton. As will be shown later, the cotton importers were originally general commission merchants, who gradually devoted more and more of their time to the cotton, and ceased dealing in other articles. But it is doubted if any generalisation of that nature can be made. If there was a tendency towards greater differentiation, it did not proceed very far for the trade as a whole, as the nature of the operations of the commission houses of the present day shows.

The Factors as Merchants. Relatively few of the commission merchants were factors solely; most of them imported or exported on their own account as well. In fact, with reference to the cotton trade, a Parliamentary Report of 1823 mentioned that "The witnesses state, that . . . there are few merchants who are not factors, and few factors who are not also merchants trading on their own account."[24] And the statements of the witnesses themselves bore out this assertion. Gabriel Shaw said that his firm was a commission house dealing in silk, wool, and cotton, but that it also imported on its own account.[25] "B" was said to be a commission merchant and also a merchant.[26]

---

[21] Parl. Papers, Report of the Lords of the Committee of Council, Dublin, 1795, p. 16.

[22] Parl. Papers, Report on Foreign Trade, 1821, VI (746), p. 294.

[23] Parl. Papers, Report on Corn Laws, 1814 (339), p. 90.
Parl. Papers, Report on Price of Foreign Grain, 1826-1827, VI (333), p. 55.

[24] Parl. Papers, Report on Merchants, 1823, p. 14.

[25] Parl. Papers, Report on Manufactures, 1833, pp. 91-92.

[26] Parl. Papers, Report on Merchants, 1823, p. 116.

Wilson, a witness before a Committee of Parliament in 1814, said:

"I am generally speaking a Corn Factor and Agent; I am not confined to be merely an Agent, I do not buy and sell on my own account in the market, but I am occasionally in the situation of principal as an importer from abroad."[27]

Hodgson, a corn dealer, asserted that he had purchased flour and grain in the United States, but that in the usual course of business he received both on consignment.[28] Gillies, another corn factor, purchased corn chiefly from the countries bordering on the Baltic and North Seas, but occasionally had corn consigned to him from the United States.[29] And finally, in the Report on the High Price of Provisions (1801) it was asserted that most of the principal factors in corn dealt on their own account, that is, they were merchants as well as commission merchants.[30]

There were, however, a number of corn factors who claimed that they never purchased corn abroad. Ruding, a corn factor, stated that "the factors' business is to sell on commission only. We do not import ourselves."[31] Nine of the witnesses who testified in 1814-1815 before the committee investigating the Corn Trade claimed that the receiving of consignments was their only business, and that they never imported on their own account.[32]

Commission Houses Trading in Both Exports and Imports. There is little evidence to indicate whether these commission merchants were to any extent importing or exporting merchants solely. An anonymous writer in 1812 said in regard to this:

"The Import and Export Trades are generally separate and are best so; either are sufficient for the capital and attention of the merchant, and by grasping at both he is often doubly a loser."[33]

[27] Parl. Papers, Report on Assize of Bread, 1814-1815, V (186), p. 268.

[28] Parl. Papers, Report on State of Agriculture, 1821, IX (668), p. 268.

[29] Parl. Papers, Report on Corn Laws, 1814 (339), p. 76.

[30] Parl. Papers, Seventh Report on High Price of Provisions, II (174), 1801, pp. 150, 155. Compare also the following:

"Are there any of the Corn factors who at present deal on their own account? Our house never does; and, I believe, it is not the practice generally of any, except those whose principal business is dealing in Corn, and who are occasionally only sellers on commissions." *Ibid.*, p. 149.

[31] Parl. Papers, Report on the Price of Foreign Grain, 1826-1827, VI (333), p. 48.

[32] Parl. Papers, Report on Grain, 1814-1815, V (26), pp. 6, 9, 11, 32, 46, 47, 53.

[33] *Matters of Fact*, 1812, p. 8.

It is not at all clear whether by "merchant" the writer referred to commission merchants, or merchants importing or exporting on their own account. While it was without question true that there were merchants who exported or imported solely, it is felt that probably most of the merchants and commission merchants combined exporting and importing.

Sir Claude Scott, a corn factor of considerable prominence, gave in 1826 testimony indicating that in the corn trade the commission merchants were not exporters as well. He was asked as to the way in which payment for corn was generally made, and answered that it was always made in specie or bills of exchange. He then continued:

"But, in many cases, the general merchant receiving cargoes of general assortments would probably receive orders to return a portion of the produce of those articles in manufactured articles, or in some other way; *but in the corn trade that has never been the practice.*"[34]

This indication that general commission merchants combined exporting and importing is strengthened by the testimony of a merchant whose knowledge of the customs of the Anglo-American trade was considerable, and whose own business was chiefly with the American markets. He stated that as a general rule merchants receiving consignments of raw produce were also exporters of British manufactured goods.[35] And we may say that the general impression which one receives from the testimony of many merchants, who described their own business operations to the different parliamentary committees, is that the British commission merchant was both an exporter and an importer.

ADVANCES ON CONSIGNMENTS

The commercial services of the commission merchant, in finding purchasers for produce consigned to Great Britain, or buying British or continental wares for foreign houses, were very important indeed, but his services in financing trade may be considered quite as important, if not more so.

Commission merchants, acting as consignees of manufacturers in England, or exporters in America or other countries, allowed

[34] Parl. Papers, Price of Foreign Grain, 1826-1827, p. 72. (Italics inserted.)

[35] Parl. Papers, Report on Commercial Distress, 1847-1848, vol. 24 (31), p. 233.

the consignor to draw bills of exchange on them at time of shipment up to two-thirds or three-fourths of the value of the consignment. The bill of exchange, when accepted by the commission merchant, was readily discounted, thus giving the consignor immediate control of funds. By the time the acceptances matured the commission merchant presumably had disposed of the goods and was in a position to pay them.

David Terni, of Ancona, a merchant in the silk trade, stated that his business consisted in shipping consignments of silk to Great Britain. He always drew against such consignments for one-half, two-thirds, or even seven-eighths of the value of the consignment.[36] Lewis Doxat said he was a commission merchant principally engaged in receiving consignments of silk from abroad. He asserted that it was his custom to make advances on the consignments of silk, after receiving the bill of lading, for about three-fourths of the value of the silk. In one year he claimed to have received £400,000 for the silk sold, and to have made advances during the same period of £250,000.[37]

A more general statement of the prevalence of the system of advances was given by a merchant in 1823. He said:

"Every man of business knows that when goods are sent for sale to this country, the consignor draws in general, at two or three months date, upon the consignee (at the time when he transmits the bills of lading) for two-thirds or three-fourths of their value."[38]

John Ewart, a commission merchant in the American trade, said that he doubted if it would be possible for consignments from America to be secured without giving such advances.[39] Another witness maintained that an invitation to consign goods to

[36] Parl. Papers, Report on Merchants, 1823, pp. 80-81.
[37] Ibid., pp. 37, 38.
[38] Ibid., p. 113. See also pp. 70, 155.
[39] Parl. Papers, Report on Manufacturers, 1833, p. 253.
"Is it usual at Liverpool for the houses of agency to advance money on account of consignments they receive? Yes.
"Is not the trade carried on in that way to a very great extent? Yes.
"As a large commission house yourself, do you believe it would be possible for any person to obtain consignments to any extent from the United States without making these advances? No; generally speaking, I do not think you could have consignments from the United States without making advances."

England was rarely sent out without an accompanying offer to make advances on the goods which might be consigned.[40]

Friedman, a Prussian merchant, claimed that at all seaports it was usual to make advances.[41] Gillies, a corn factor, asserted that it was the "universal practice" for the consignor to draw against consignments of corn.[42] Andrew Loughnan, a commission merchant in the Spanish wool trade, who was constantly receiving consignments of wool, claimed that it was almost uniformly the rule for the consignors of wool to draw bills of exchange against the consignments.[43] George Larpent, of the firm of Paxton, Cockerell, Nail and Company, stated that it was the "invariable practice" to draw against consignments of cotton and other produce from the East Indies from one-half to two-thirds of their invoice value, and independent of the charges to be paid in England for freight, commissions, etc.[44]

This evidence would lead us to the conclusion that the system of advances on consignments was an integral part of the commission business, and prevailed almost universally in all lines of trade.

COMMISSIONS

There were many expenses connected with the receiving of consignments which the commission merchant had to defray. Manifestly, he was reimbursed for such expenses, and he received besides, as compensation for his services, a commission or factorage based on the selling price of the goods, or the invoice price plus the charges which he himself had met. In some cases, though it was not customary, this commission was reckoned at so much per cask or other package. Harvey, a corn factor, said the usual commission on corn was one shilling per sack in 1814;[45]

[40] Parl. Papers, Report on Merchants, p. 91.
[41] *Ibid.*, p. 48.
[42] *Ibid.*, p. 42.
[43] *Ibid.*, 1823, p. 41.
[44] *Ibid.*, p. 49.
When a factor advanced on goods consigned to him, or paid the freight or other incidental charges, a lien attached to the goods entrusted to him for sale. If the goods were sold then he had a lien upon the sale price, and had the right to enforce payment of the money to himself, in opposition to the claims of the principal, provided he served notice of his claim upon the debtor before payment was made to his principal. Chitty, *Treatise*, 1824, III, p. 211.
[45] Parl. Papers, Report on Assize of Bread, 1814-1815, V (186), p. 80.

while in 1801 it was stated that a commission per quarter was charged, and, in addition, a percentage on the value.[46]

The rate of commission charged ranged from two to five per cent, depending largely on the country in which the goods were bought or sold. The following table gives the rates which were common in Europe and America at the opening of the nineteenth century:

Rates of Commission.

	In Europe	Charged by European merchants to correspondents in West Indies and United States.	Charged by U. S. and W. I. commission merchants to European correspondents.
1. Purchase of goods	2% on invoice	2½%	5%
2. Sale of goods	2% on amt.	2½%	5%
3. *Del credere*	2% " "	2½%	5%
4. Effecting insurance on ships or goods	½% on amt. insured	2½%	5%
5. Recovery of losses on ships or goods insured	2% on sum recovered	2½%	5%
6. Accepting bills for foreign account	½%	2½%	5%
7. Receiving and paying for money for foreign account	½%		5%
8. Remitting bills			5%
9. Acting as attorney for recovery of property			5%

10. Commission paid by manufacturers to their factors or agents 5% on the amount of the goods they sell for their account, including warehouse rent and *del credere*.[47]

The third item in the above table, called "*del credere*" referred to a commission charged by a commission merchant to compensate him for assuming the risk of payment by the vendee. In other words, when a commission house sold produce for a merchant and charged the *del credere* commission, it guaranteed the payment of the account.

In the linen trade *del credere* was reckoned at one per cent,[48]

[46] Parl. Papers, Seventh Report on High Price of Provisions, 1801, p. 148.

[47] Montefiore, *Commercial Dict.*, 1804, I, p. 474.

[48] Parl. Papers, Report of Linen, 1822, VII (560), p. 79.

while in the corn trade it ranged from 1d. to 4½d. in the pound sterling according to the financial standing of the miller,[49] although it was asserted that at Hull it was reckoned at four per cent.[50] The guarantee of the payment of accounts was a familiar practice both in Great Britain and in America, and applied to all lines of business, domestic and foreign.[51]

THE IMPORTANCE OF COMMISSION MERCHANTS

Probably the commission merchant was the most important figure in the foreign trade organisation of both the United States and Great Britain. Certainly the statement will hold true if we consider as commission merchants all those who dealt at all as factors.

In America the cotton trade and the produce trade were largely in the hands of the commission merchants;[52] and after 1815 the greater proportion of British manufactures was consigned to commission merchants of one sort or another.[53] In the list of business cards or advertisements in the *New Orleans Price Current* for October 7, 1848, we find 343 firms advertising as commission merchants of one description or another, while there are only a very few firms of any other type advertising.[54] The census of 1840 listed 381 commission houses in Louisiana, as contrasted with 24 commercial houses engaged in foreign trade.[55] The same census gave for the State of New York 1,044 commission houses, and 469 commercial houses.[56] Yet in Massachusetts there were 241 commercial houses in the foreign trade, as contrasted with 123 commission houses.[57]

Evidence of the importance of the commission house in Great

---

[49] Parl. Papers, Report on Assize of Bread, 1814-1815, p. 80.

[50] Parl. Papers, Report on the Price of Foreign Grain, 1826-1827, p. 46.

[51] Parl. Papers, Report on Manufactures, 1833, p. 205. Hunt, *Merchants' Magazine*, 1847, vol. XVII, p. 164.

"It is a familiar practice with them [commission merchants] to sell goods on what is called a *del credere* commission, that is, a percentage, in consideration of which they undertake to be liable to their consignor for the price of the goods, in case and when the buyer fails to pay."

[52] *Vide* Chapter IV.

[53] *Vide* Chapter VI.

[54] *New Orleans Price Current*, October 7, 1848.

[55] Compendium of . . . Sixth Census, 1841, p. 237.

[56] *Ibid.*, p. 129.

[57] *Ibid.*, p. 105.

Britain is implicit in all the previous discussion, but there are certain generalisations regarding the commission house which seem worth quoting. One witness stated that the trade of Liverpool was chiefly in the hands of the commission houses.

"Is not the trade of Liverpool principally commission houses? Yes, it is, generally speaking."[58]

And he reaffirmed and supplemented that given above:

"Is the business of the merchants at Liverpool done principally on their own account or for others? There is a great deal of agency there."
"Is the agency business at Liverpool chiefly in the hands of comparatively few merchants or very large capital and connections? No; it is very generally diffused."[59]

Lord Liverpool is said to have estimated that two-thirds of the entire trade of Great Britain was carried on by the commission merchants.

"And he might say that he believed that two thirds of the whole commerce of the country was carried on by consigning goods to a factor, and leaving it to his discretion to dispose of them to the greatest advantage, sending them to market when he pleased, and raising money on them when he could not send them to market."[60]

BROKERS

DEFINITION

The broker was an agent transacting business for a principal, and in that respect very similar to a factor. The chief point of difference between a broker and a factor was that the factor had possession of the goods, and made contracts in his own name which were binding on the principal, whereas the broker did not have possession of the goods, nor the right to sell in his own name, but acted merely as the intermediary between the principals.[61]

"Factors and brokers are, in some respects, nearly identical, but in others they are radically different. 'A factor,' said Mr. Justice Hol-

[58] Parl. Papers, Report on Manufactures, 1833, p. 251.
[59] *Ibid.*, p. 253.
[60] McCulloch, *Dictionary*, 1834, p. 571. Quoted from a speech in the House of Lords.
[61] Chitty, *Treatise*, III, 1824, p. 193.

royd, in a late case, 'differs materially from a broker. The former is a person to whom goods are sent or consigned; and he has not only the possession, but, in consequence of its being usual to advance money upon them, has also a special property in them, and a general lien upon them. When, therefore, he sells in his own name, it is within the scope of his authority; and it may be right, therefore, that the principal should be bound by the consequences of such sale. But the case of a broker is different; he has not the possession of the goods, and so the vendor cannot be deceived by the circumstance; and besides, the employing a person to sell goods as a broker does not authorise him to sell in his own name. If, therefore, he sells in his own name, he acts beyond the scope of his authority; and his principal is not bound.' "[62]

The brokers of the city of London were the subject of regulation from the time of Edward I on.[63] They were required to be licensed by the Lord Mayor and aldermen, for which a fee of £5 was charged, as well as a yearly payment of £5. A medal was given the licensed broker, with his name engraved thereon, which he might produce if required as evidence of his qualification.[64] Persons found to be acting as brokers without having been sworn in and licensed were subject to a fine of £100. Some of the regulations established by the mayor and aldermen pursuant to the statute 8 and 9 Will. 3. c. 20 were that every person upon his admission, should take an oath truly and faithfully to execute and perform the office of broker between party and party, in all things pertaining to the duty of his office, without fraud or collusion, to the best of his ability; that he should in all cases

[62] McCulloch, *Dictionary*, 1834, p. 568. Compare also the following definitions of a broker:

"Brokers, as well as factors, are agents, but they differ in this respect: the broker settles the contract between merchant and merchant, the factor not only contracts, but he sells and buys in execution of the contracts he has made.

"Whether the object of agreement be merchandise or stock, the go-between is a broker." Caines, *Lex. Merc. Am.*, 1802, p. 419.

"A broker is a person employed as an intermediate or mutual agent, who by avowedly not acting for himself, or upon his own responsibility, serves as a witness to the contracts between the two parties." Tate, *Elements*, 1819, I, p. 117.

"The broker . . . is not ordinarily trusted with possession of the goods, and ought not to sell in his own name and receive the purchase money." Edwards, *Factors and Brokers*, 1870, p. 25.

[63] *Bankers' Magazine* (London), 1847, vol. VII, p. 329.

[64] McCulloch, *Dictionary*, 1834, p. 187. (Gives Montefiore's *Com. Dict.* as authority.)

reveal the name of his principal, and neither deal in goods on his own account nor barter and sell again, nor make any gain in goods beyond the usual brokerage; and that he should regularly register all the contracts into which he entered. A broker was further required to give a bond of £500 for the faithful performance of the duties of the office.

The law and the regulations established in conformity to the law appear to have been much more rigorous than the actuality, for unsworn brokers were said to be very numerous.

"We are aware that the number of Brokers admitted and sworn of the city of London, agreeably to the law of the 6th of Anne, and 57th of George III amounts to more than 1,300; but this only proves that men will act as Brokers contrary to existing laws . . . and all this in face of a penalty of £100 for each offence. Let any Tradesman in actual business consult the list which hangs on the North side of the Royal Exchange, and he will discover about one name in four of these he may know who practice as Brokers, Appraisers, Etc."[65]

The broker was also enjoined from dealing in merchandise or produce on his own account, but there seems to have been little attention paid to this regulation. An anonymous writer said of this:

"A broker is restricted, by the terms of his bond, from speculating on his own behalf; but little regard is paid to the supposed injunction, and scarcely an individual ever entered the markets who has not infringed the law in this respect. . . .

"The broker can always ease his conscience from being his own 'principal,' by substituting the name of anybody else he chooses."[66]

CLASSES OF BROKERS

Some of the brokers were general brokers, handling any goods that might be entrusted to them for sale. The firm of Trueman and Cook, of London, offers an example of this type of broker. It did not confine its attention to any one article, but sold cotton, spices, sugar, coffee, indigo, etc. The volume of business transacted by it was very large indeed. "Such is the extent of their operations, that it is said, they dispose of produce of the worth of several millions of money in the course of the year.[67]

65 *The London Tradesman*, 1819, p. 76, note.
66 *The City*, 1845, pp. 180-181.
67 *Ibid.*, p. 183.

Mr. Cook gave an account of his business when he testified in 1833.

"About two thirds of a million pounds sterling of the sugar exported from the island of Mauritius, and which arrives in this port, pass through my hands. I sell it for the account of the different consignees resident in London, and guarantee the proceeds; the importer having nothing to do with the receipt of the sugar from the buyers, they hold me responsible; I give the credit and account to them for the proceeds. We are the agents entrusted with the property for sale."[68]

If one can judge from the advertisements in the newspapers of the day, most of the brokers of Liverpool were general brokers in that they handled more than one article, but there seems to have been a certain limitation on the articles handled. For example, Park and Fletcher advertised sales at auction of potashes, hides, turpentine, tar, lemon juice, skins, indigo, lumber, and wool; Colin Campbell advertised horn tips, shank bones, barrel staves, cotton, and apples; Percival and Barton offered sugar, molasses, and ginger.[69] In other words, there appears to have been a specialisation among the brokers paralleling the specialisation of the commission merchants, who confined themselves to goods from a particular market. And in the case of individual firms we find this to be true. Kymor, M'Taggart and Company, for example, described themselves as brokers in West India produce. They were important figures in their trade, for they claimed to make advances of £250,000 annually.[70] Thomas Kemble, Son and Company likewise specialised in West India produce,[71] and there were brokers in American, East India, or South American produce as well.

In many cases, however, brokers handled only certain specific articles. There were tea, tallow, coffee, sugar, spice, or wool brokers; agents whose operations were restricted to the selling or buying of one or another of these articles. In the cotton trade, with the growth in the volume of cotton handled, there arose a large class of brokers who specialised solely in cotton.[72] Apparently the same was true in the wool trade.[73]

[68] Parl. Papers, Report on Manufactures, 1833, p. 98.
[69] *Liverpool Mercury*, July-December, 1820.
[70] Parl. Papers, Report on Merchants, 1823, p. 103.
[71] *Ibid.*, p. 105.
[72] *Vide* Chapter III.
[73] Parl. Papers, Report on British Wool Trade, 1828, VIII (515), p. 79.
Whether there were brokers in all lines of trade is impossible to deter-

THE OPERATIONS OF A BROKER

When a merchant informed a broker that he wished to buy so many bales of cotton or so many hundred-weight of sugar, the broker went to market to interview other brokers, in order to find out the price of the day, and where the desired produce might be obtained. If the merchant had not given him a maximum price which he might pay, he informed him of the price at which the cotton or sugar could be procured. When the terms of purchase were approved by the merchant, and the purchase arranged, it was then the broker's duty to make a note of the purchase in a book of his own, stating the names of the buyer and seller, the quality and description of the article bought, the price for which it was bought, and any special or unusual conditions or terms of purchase. Having made this note, he signed it, and went to the selling broker to compare it with a similar note made by him. If the notes corresponded exactly, the buying broker sent an exact copy of his memorandum to the broker of the seller, whose duty it was to exchange it for an exact copy of his own memorandum. Each copy was, or should have been, signed by the broker who sent it. They were then called "bought and sold notes," the bought note being that which was sent to the seller's broker. If the same broker acted for both the buyer and seller, after making the entry in his book it was his duty— and it was generally the practice—to call on both parties to the transaction, in order to ascertain that he had made his entry correctly, according to the views of both parties. He then sent a copy of the memorandum to buyer and seller.[74]

Of the value of these "bought and sold" notes as evidence in case of litigation, Tate remarked:

". . . in all engagements or contracts to purchase or dispose of property, whether they are verbal or written, when a sworn Broker is

mine. In the advertisements in the *Liverpool Mercury*, already noted, an extraordinarily large number of articles of colonial produce was mentioned. But in the corn trade, and possibly in other lines as well, the broker does not appear to have been of any importance. The factor dealt directly with the miller without any go-between. Wilson, a Corn Factor, was questioned on this point:

"Are the London Corn Factors . . . what you would call Corn Brokers? I conceive there is no such thing as a Corn Broker." Parl. Papers, Report on Assize of Bread, 1814-1815, p. 36.

74 *Bankers' Magazine* (New York), vol. VIII, March, 1854, p. 755. Adapted from "Foreign Items—The Broker Business."

employed, his official notice, called a contract note, to the party to whom the contract is to be rendered binding, with his entry of the particulars in a book, which it is a part of his duty to keep, has the same effect, in case of a litigation, as would attend a written agreement stamped and witnessed; . . ."[75]

As the effect of a contract thus made was so binding, in order to prevent any mistakes in the agreement, it was provided that the party against whom it would operate should have a reasonable time to give it consideration. This was considered to be until the opening of business on the next morning, and if the contract note was then returned, no legal claim existed against him.[76] In cases where credit was involved and payments were to be made by a bill of exchange, the law allowed the seller longer time to consider the solvency of the vendee, and in a decision handed down by Lord Ellenborough, it was decided that five days was not too long a period for making the necessary inquiries.[77]

Most of the sales originally negotiated by the brokers seem to have been private sales, but in a number of lines the custom arose of selling merchandise at public auction. These auctions were held to a certain extent in the rooms of the brokers, and buying and selling were in the hands of the brokers exclusively.

"The term *broker,* therefore, appears at first sight strictly to include only negotiators of private treaties; but since the custom has sprung up in particular trades of systematically adopting the medium of public sales for the disposal of merchandise, many brokers in the city of London have assumed also the character of auctioneers, being licenced both under the excise laws as well as by the civic authorities.

"The custom at first sight, appears to have been that these public sales, which are generally conducted in rooms belonging to brokers, were mere meetings among the brokers themselves, where each broker in turn was enabled at one meeting to dispose of various lots of goods which were entrusted to him for sale, among such of his fellow brokers as were commissioned to purchase; and then gradually rose up the vast transactions which are daily taking place in Mincing Lane and other markets of the city."[78]

Contrary to the usual custom, the broker assumed the charac-

[75] Tate, *Elements,* 1819, vol. I, p. 117.
[76] *Ibid.,* p. 117.
[77] McCulloch, *Dictionary,* 1834, p. 187.
[78] *Bankers' Magazine* (London), 1847, vol. VII, p. 329.

ter of a principal at auction sales, and became, in fact if not at law, responsible for the payments of a defaulting principal.

"In the public sales of goods only sworn brokers can legally officiate, and such has become the custom of trade, that at all the principal public sales, particularly those of the East India Company, none but brokers bid for the articles to be sold; any other person certainly possesses the right of so doing, but from the competition he would create, his interests would suffer a material injury. Hence in public sales, brokers act as principals, and a disclosure of real purchasers and sellers is seldom made; the brokers becoming completely responsible for the due performance of the conditions of the sale."[79]

One of the public salesrooms was known as the Commercial Salerooms in Mincing Lane, and was said to have been a great resort of the produce brokers.

"The Commercial Sale-rooms in Mincing-lane are the great resort of these gentry [the produce brokers], where apartments have been specially fitted up for the sales of tea, sugar, coffee, spices, and the other description of articles, coming within the category of 'foreign and colonial' produce. These sale-rooms are nicely arranged with seats for the 'buyers,' a rostrum for the 'seller,' and a side-desk for his clerk to check prices. At the tea and sugar sales the attendance is often as many as one hundred and one hundred and fifty persons, all armed with catalogues and pens, making their 'bids,' as the market or article suits them."[80]

The principal days for these sales at auction were Tuesday and Friday, when large quantities of produce of all descriptions were disposed of. The sales began at ten or eleven in the morning, and did not conclude before three or four in the afternoon.[81]

ADVANCES TO COMMISSION MERCHANTS

The interlacing of credits is one of the interesting features of trade in general. In the foreign trade in this period we found it customary for the factor to make advances to the merchant, and we shall now see that it was usual for the broker to make advances to the factor, and in many cases for the broker to get advances from the banker. Again, as will be shown later in Chapter V, the manufacturer secured advances from the commission

---

[79] Tate, *Elements*, 1819, vol. I, pp. 117, 118.
[80] *The City*, 1845, p. 178.
[81] *Ibid.*, p. 182.

merchant, and the commission merchant often sought advances from another commission merchant, and so on until the goods were finally sold and paid for. The entire capital of the nation thus was placed at the disposal of those engaged in purveying goods to local or foreign customers.

Evidence showing the general prevalence of this custom is very abundant. Elsewhere we shall discuss in detail the relation of the cotton broker to the cotton merchant in the matter of advances. At this point we wish to show that in other lines also the system was well established.

Speaking of the general custom of giving credits to the consignor of goods, a witness noted, in 1823, that the bills, drawn for the purpose of securing the advances, frequently fell due before the goods were sold, or before payment was made. At such times, if the funds of the merchant were low, and his stock of goods large, he applied to his broker for a sum of money on account of the sales, or to his banker, who would ''advance on the brokers' bill or engage to pay the same out of the proceeds as they are received.''[82]

Another witness, testifying a bit later, gave a very complete picture of the way in which advances were secured from the broker.

"There are two kinds of Bills drawn against Produce: the first is the original Bill drawn abroad upon the Merchant, who imports it. In consequence of the Steamer the Bills which are drawn against Produce frequently fall due before the Steamer arrives. The Merchant, therefore, when it arrives, if he has not sufficient Capital has to pledge that Produce with the Broker till he has Time to sell that Produce. Then a new Species of Bill is immediately drawn by the Merchant in Liverpool upon the Broker on the Security of that Produce lodged in the Warehouse in Liverpool, bonded or free. Then it is the business of the Banker to ascertain from the Broker whether he has the Produce and to what extent he has advanced upon it. It is his business to see that the Broker has Property to protect himself if he make a loss."[83]

A method of making advances which was said to have been quite common in Liverpool, was for the commission merchant to turn over the bill of lading to the broker, leaving him to pay the freight and other charges incidental to the safe custody and

---

[82] Parl. Papers, Report on Merchants, 1823, p. 113.
[83] Parl. Papers, Report on Commercial Distress, 1847-1848, XXIV (31), p. 283.

sale of the goods, and allowing him to reimburse himself for these advances from the proceeds of the sale.[84]

Some of the brokers were particularly active in securing business for themselves by offering their services in helping the importers financially. The activities of one of these eager brokers were described as follows:

"Suppose a broker of this description finds a merchant, for whom he does business, entered in the Customs Reports as the party to whom 60,000 bags of Mauritius sugar, or any other produce of considerable value, is consigned; he immediately goes to him, and inquires if he be in need of any advance. Should assistance be required, he is ready to provide the money, upon the deposit of the warrants for the goods; and while securing for his advance the rate of two-and-a-quarter, or two-and-a-half per cent., as may be the currency of Lombard-street discounts, the one-half per cent. commission for sale must follow when the goods are offered at auction."[85]

The importance of the financial assistance of the brokers and bankers to the commission merchants was clearly indicated in the report of the committee investigating the state of the merchants in 1823.

"Your Committee have been convinced, not only from the concurring testimony of the witnesses in general, but from the evidence of an eminent banker in particular as well as that of brokers for bills and merchandise that the extensive advances made upon goods consigned to this country for sale during the last twenty or thirty years, whilst our foreign trade has been so greatly extended, have been furnished in a considerable degree by bankers, brokers, and other capitalists who have lent money largely to the merchants on the security of their merchandise, or of brokers' acceptances and engagements, secured on such merchandise."[86]

In the produce trade in particular, it was noticed that the capital resources of the brokers made it possible for them to be of great importance in financing that trade.

"The chief of the brokerage business in produce is getting into the hands of one or two large houses, which is accounted for by the command of capital they enjoy. It is a question, whether the manner in which they have of late years transacted their trade, has not invested them with powers equal to our best bankers and discounters. Three of

[84] Parl. Papers, Report on Merchants, 1823, p. 110.
[85] *The City*, 1845, p. 177.
[86] Parl. Papers, Report on Merchants, 1823, p. 17.

the largest produce-brokers in this metropolis maintain much of their business by the enormous advances they make to merchants on their consignments. Having gained a strong reputation by the extent of their business, they can as readily get money from the Bank of England on their own bills, as any of the bankers and merchants themselves. In such a situation they are almost able to act as they think fit with their customers."[87]

This general readiness of the broker to advance money to the commission merchant led many of them into difficulties and some of them to disaster, for the British law did not allow the factor to pledge the goods of his principal for a loan to himself.

"A factor cannot pledge the goods of his principal; therefore, where goods were consigned from abroad to a factor to be sold on account of the consignor, and a bill of lading was sent to deliver the goods to the factor or his assigns, and the factor afterwards indorsed and delivered the bill of lading, together with the goods, to the defendants, as brokers, with instructions to do the needful; and the defendants made advances to him, on the credit of those and other goods, without knowing that he was not the owner of them: Held,—that the defendants could not retain the goods against the consignor until payment of the debt due to them from the factor on account of their advances."[88]

The opinions of certain of the justices of England on this subject were given in the Report on Merchants. Some of these are given below to show more clearly the legal position of the broker who had made advances to the commission merchant.

"A factor has no right under any circumstances, to pledge the goods of his principal for his own benefit." Mr. Justice Bailey.
"It is a rule established by the common law that a factor cannot pledge, and bind his principal by it. He may sell, and then his principal will be bound. Mere possession of property will not pass the right to dispose of it as the factor pleases. He has a limited trust which he cannot exceed to the prejudice of his principal." Mr. Justice Holroyd.[89]

In this report a number of cases were cited in which the brokers had been ruined by the failure of the factor, and although they had the possession of the goods on which they had made

[87] *The City*, 1845, p. 177.
[88] Parl. Papers, Report on Merchants, 1823, p. 184. Quoted from Martin vs. Coles and others, I Maule and Selwyn, 140: Hilary Term, 1813, Friday, February 5th.
[89] *Ibid.*, p. 61. Quoted from "Duclos vs. Ryland, 5th Moore's Reports."

advances, they could not hold them against the demands of the merchant who had consigned them to the factor.

For example, a foreign house consigned three cargoes of wheat to a London merchant "A," who placed them in the hands of "B" for sale. "A" made large advances to the foreign merchant, and after waiting for fifteen months, wanted payment or permission to sell. The foreign house then got "W" to pay off "A's" advances and "B" was again placed in charge of the sales. "W" asked and received advances from "B." Before the sale had been consummated "W" became bankrupt, the foreign house claimed the wheat, and "B" lost £848.[90]

Many similar cases might be cited, but it is felt that the above case is sufficient to exemplify the position of the broker. It is a curious fact that in spite of such possibilities of loss, the custom of giving advances should have continued and have been so widespread. Apparently few of the brokers realised exactly the position in which they placed themselves until the Parliamentary Committee began to make its investigations.[91] The publicity given to the legal standing of the broker by this inquiry, and the fact that this law obtained only in Great Britain and the United States, made it necessary or at least advisable to change the law so as to protect the broker.[92]

By a law passed in 1826 (6 Geo. 4. c. 94), the position of the broker was made much more secure, for all persons entrusted with and in the possession of goods were supposed, unless the contrary were made distinctly to appear, to be their owners, so far, at least, that they were allowed to pledge them or sell them to third parties.[93]

COMMISSIONS

The broker, as well as the factor, was paid on a commission basis—a certain percentage on the value of the goods which he bought or sold. In some cases the brokerage was a particular charge on each article sold, and not a percentage. The seller of the article usually paid the commission, and the brokers were

[90] Parl. Papers, Report on Merchants, 1823, p. 65.

[91] J. Martin, a banker, said in 1823 that until 1810 few brokers had any realisation of the danger which they had been running in making advances. Parl. Papers, Report on Merchants, 1823, p. 121.

[92] Parl. Papers, Report on Merchants, 1823, p. 66. McCulloch, *Dict.*, 1834, p. 571.

[93] McCulloch, *Dict.*, 1834, p. 572.

not supposed to secure compensation from both sides; in fact, this double brokerage was distinctly forbidden in London. Tate remarked, however, that when a purchaser commissioned him to search the market for the particular good which he wanted, the broker had a right to make him a charge for the extra trouble, but that it was usual for the seller also to allow him a commission of one-half per cent, or the regular allowance, "as a douceur for bringing him a customer."[94]

The regular charges for brokerage varied from one-tenth of one per cent to one per cent. It was stated that the commission allowed to produce brokers was, on the average, one-half of one per cent, although on certain articles one per cent was allowed, "but these are few indeed." In the cotton trade the brokerage varied from one-half of one per cent to one per cent at different times during the first half of the nineteenth century.[95]

Many of the brokers guaranteed the sales for the commission merchant, and in such cases an extra commission for *del credere* was charged.[96] A broker and commission merchant stated in 1833 that earlier about one-fourth of the brokerage business was guaranteed, but with the increase of trade the custom of charging *del credere* had decreased, the merchants or the commission merchants themselves assuming the risk of nonpayment by the vendee.[97]

BROKERS IN AMERICA

The existence in the American trade organisation of a class of brokers as important to the trade as were the British brokers seems very doubtful. Merchandise brokers did exist, and we are informed that, contrary to the custom prevailing in Great Britain, the American brokers were not required to be licensed nor to give bonds.[98] *The Boston Almanac* for 1850 listed twenty-three merchandise and produce brokers in Boston.[99] In 1823 Kayser's *Commercial Directory* noted in Boston only four brokers who without question dealt in merchandise, and mentioned none in New York, although certain brokers were listed who

[94] Tate, *Elements*, 1819, vol. I, p. 119.
[95] *The City*, 1845, p. 176.
[96] Tate, *Elements*, 1819, vol. I, p. 119.
[97] Parl. Papers, Report on Manufactures, 1833, p. 246.
[98] *Encycl. Americana*, 1830, vol. II, p. 279
[99] *Boston Almanac*, 1850.

may or may not have been merchandise brokers.[100] In an issue of the *New Orleans Price Current*, the advertisements of only three merchandise brokers, two tobacco brokers, and one merchandise and produce broker were found out of a total of nearly four hundred advertisements of commission merchants and forwarding merchants.[101]

We hesitate to generalise on the subject because of lack of really trustworthy references on the activity and importance of the broker. Yet, on the other hand, this very fact that the American brokers do not seem to have made a great impression on their contemporaries, leads us to the tentative conclusion that they were of minor importance in the trade organisation of this period.

[100] Kayser, *Commercial Directory*, 1823, pp. 87-95 and pp. 139-145.
[101] *New Orleans Price Current*, January 19, 1848.

CHAPTER III

THE BRITISH COTTON MARKET

A STUDY of the handling of raw cotton in Great Britain must necessarily include a survey of the great market of Liverpool. In fact, Liverpool so overshadows the other markets in Great Britain that it has seemed profitable to confine the discussion to the organisation of the Liverpool market.

At present, one is accustomed to think of Liverpool as the great primary cotton market of the world, a market influencing profoundly all the other markets for that commodity, reflecting the changes in any particular market, and passing them on to the other markets; in short, a focal point for the play of all the intricate forces of supply and demand in cotton the world over. It would not be far from the truth to say that this has been the case always, yet the statement cannot be made without qualification.

In the first place, it is obvious that a century and more ago no market could so sensitively register the temporary ebbs and flows in the various other primary and secondary markets as does the market of Liverpool today. It is only with the increasing complexity and efficiency of organisation, and, above all, with the improvements in the means of transportation, and in the collection and dissemination of information, that we find really a world market, with Liverpool as the central point.

But aside from that Liverpool did not definitely establish her leadership in the importation of cotton until in the nineteenth century. London and Glasgow were of importance in the quarter of a century before 1800. The following figures of the total importations of cotton into the United Kingdom and the importations into Liverpool for about the first ten years of the nineteenth century show the increasing importance of Liverpool as a port of entry for cotton.

Year	Total importations of cotton into the U. K.	Importations of cotton into Liverpool
	(In bales or bags)[1]	
1802	281,383	135,192
1803	238,898	140,291
1804	242,610	153,126
1805	252,620	177,508
1806	261,738	173,074
1807	282,667	196,467
1808	168,138	66,215
1809	440,382	267,283
1810	561,173	320,594
1811	326,231	174,132
1812	261,205	171,551[2]

[1] In the account given it is not specified as to whether the figures are in bags or bales. But the determination of the exact unit is not considered a point of fundamental importance. It is the comparison of Liverpool with other ports that concerns us.

It is worth noting that the figures in the second column, with minor differences, correspond to the figures given by Smithers (*Liverpool*, p. 147), suggesting an official source common to both accounts. Smithers' table is given in 'packages.'

The terms 'package,' 'bale,' and 'bag,' seem, in this period, to be used with a great deal of freedom. In fact, I doubt very much if any clear distinction can be made between the different terms. In support of this statement I quote below an extract from a report made in 1836 by Secretary of the Treasury Woodbury (A report on the Cultivation, Manufacture, and Foreign Trade of Cotton, p. 30). It is a preface to certain cotton statistics which he gives and a justification for quoting the statistics in pounds rather than in bales. Secretary Woodbury said:

". . . it appears that in 1790 the bale or bag in the United States was computed at only 200 pounds (see Treasury Report, 15th February, 1791). In the Atlantic States it is now estimated often at 300 and 324 pounds, but in those on the Gulf of Mexico at 400 or 450 pounds. Those used at Lowell in 1831 contained on the average 361 pounds (Pitkin's *Statistics*, p. 527, note). At Liverpool the Sea Island bale was, a few years ago. estimated at 280 pounds, and the Upland at 320 pounds. The bales imported into France are estimated at 300 pounds each, by Burns, *History of Cotton*, p. 525. In 1824 all the bales imported into Liverpool averaged 266 pounds, and increased yearly until in 1832 they weighed on an average, 319 pounds (McCulloch, p. 441), though on the previous page he considers from 300 to 310 pounds a fair average, and Burns, cited on the same page, makes it 310 pounds in 1832. The Egyptian bale contained once only 90 pounds; the Brazilian, 180 pounds (Pitk. 485); the West Indian, 350 pounds; and the Columbia bale or quintal, 101 pounds (Cyclop. of ·Com.). In 1832 Burns says the average of the United States bale or bag imported into England was 345 pounds; Brazilian, 180 pounds; Egyptian, 220 pounds; West Indian, 300 pounds; East Indian, 330 pounds (McCulloch, 441)."

Two things are very noticeable in the above quotation; in the first place, the very great difference in the weight of a bale of cotton, and in the second, the use of the terms 'bale' and 'bag' as referring to the same thing.

[2] *Liverpool Mercury*, February 5, 1813, p. 254.

It will be seen that in 1802 about forty-eight per cent of the total imports came in through Liverpool; in 1812, about sixty-five per cent of the cotton was imported into Liverpool. As the total imports became greater in volume the position of Liverpool as the centre of the cotton trade became more marked. In 1823 it was stated that a total of 187,231,520 pounds of cotton was imported into Great Britain; of this total, 25,238,360 pounds were imported into London and Glasgow, and the balance, 161,-993,160 pounds, was imported into Liverpool. In other words Liverpool imported approximately eighty-seven per cent of the total.[3] Baines has stated the importations of cotton in 1833 to have been as follows:

Cotton imported into	Bags
Liverpool	840,953
London	40,350
Glasgow	48,913
Total	930,216[4]

This means that Liverpool received over ninety per cent of the cotton imported in that year. The explanation of this control of the cotton trade by Liverpool rests doubtless on the growing concentration of the cotton industry in Manchester and the surrounding neighborhood.

It is, I think, worth noticing that the expansion of the commerce of Liverpool is largely associated with the American trade, both exporting and importing. In 1808 Mr. Alexander Baring, a merchant of wide experience in American trade, stated that Liverpool was the principal centre of the American commerce, the function of the London houses being to act almost solely as bankers for the American trade, receiving the proceeds of consignments from America to all parts of the world, and paying the drafts of merchants to the order of the British manufacturers.[5] Not only was Liverpool important as the centre of American trade in Great Britain, but the American trade was probably the most important single trade which the

[3] Smithers, *Liverpool*, 1825, p. 143.
[4] Baines, *Cotton Manufacture*, 1835, p. 318.
[5] Baring, *Inquiry*, 1808, p. 7.

merchants of Liverpool carried on. Mr. Rathbone, a merchant of Liverpool, stated in evidence in 1808, that he believed the American trade comprised about five-sixteenths of the whole trade of Liverpool.[6]

In the period before 1795, the exports of American cotton to Great Britain were insignificant in amount, and in all probability were to a great extent reëxportations. It was stated that among the exports of "Charles Town" from November, 1747, to November, 1748, were included 'seven bags of cotton wool valued at 3£ 11s. 5d. per bag,' and in 1754 mention was made of the export of 'some cotton' from South Carolina.[7] In Brooke's account of Liverpool, he says,

"An account of the imports of merchandise from all places into Liverpool in 1770 has fortunately been preserved, and amongst other articles the importation of cotton was then as follows:

From New York	3 bales
" Virginia and Maryland	4 bags
" North Carolina	3 bbls.
" Georgia	3 bags."[8]

That America had not exported cotton of domestic origin, and was not considered as likely to become a cotton exporting country, is well illustrated by an incident, occurring in 1784, when eight bags of cotton, imported in an American ship from the United States into Liverpool, were seized by an officer of the customs under an impression that the cotton could not be the growth of the United States, and hence could not legally be carried to Great Britain in a ship in the registry of the United States.[9]

6 Parl. Papers, Minutes of Evidence on Petitions of Merchants in Liverpool, 1808 (119), p. 76.

7 Seabrook, *Memoir on the Origin, Cultivation and Uses of Cotton*, 1844, p. 12.

8 Brooke, *Liverpool*, 1853, p. 244. Quoted from Enfield's *Leverpool*, pp. 73, 74, 79.

9 *Ibid.*, p. 243. This incident is referred to in almost every work on the cotton plant. Brooke gives as his authority *Recollections of Liverpool*, published anonymously, but—he says—written by Bryan Blundell and published in February, 1824. Brooke's father, who was living at the time in Liverpool, confirmed the story.

In this connection Brooke remarked,

"But another remarkable circumstance connected with those eight bags of cotton remains to be told. It would seem that the importation of the eight bags caused something like a glut in the market, because they lay in the warehouse of Messrs. William Rathbone and Sons, who were the consignees of them, for several months, for want of buyers, and were afterwards sold to Messrs. Strutt and Co. of Derby."[10]

In the year 1785 five bags, and in 1786 six bags only of American cotton were imported. In 1791 the imports had jumped to sixty-four bags, and in 1795 to over two thousand. By 1795 the cotton gin had sufficiently demonstrated its utility to make it worth while to plant larger acreage to cotton. It is interesting to note that the exports in 1794 were but 348 bags, showing an increase in one year of over 500 per cent.[11]

In the early stages of the cotton industry, the raw cotton used in Great Britain, in the coarse goods, was the growth principally of the West Indies;[12] the finer sorts came from Surinam, the Brazils, and the Isle of Bourbon.[13] A certain amount, never apparently of much importance, was imported from Turkey. In 1791 the following sources were given for the imports into Liverpool:

[10] Brooke, *op. cit.*, p. 244. This account is supposed to have been communicated to the author by Mr. William Rathbone, whose father and grandfather were the above-mentioned firm.

[11] Smithers, *Liverpool*, p. 129, 147.

[12] Enfield gave the following account of the total cotton importations into Liverpool in 1770. It illustrates the marked importance of the West Indies as a source of cotton:

American Colonies	3 bales, 7 bags, 3 bbls.
West Indies—Antigua	168 bags
Barbadoes	459 "
Dominque	705 "
Granada	1,083 "
Jamaica	1,775 "
St. Kitts	100 "
Montserat	178 "
Tostola	949 "
St. Vincents	610 "
Total	6,027 "

—Enfield, *Leverpool*, 1774, pp. 73-79.

[13] Smithers, *Liverpool*, p. 123.

Country	Packages
Portugal	34,500
Holland	1,950
Turkey	2,242
America	64
West India	25,777
Ireland	3,871
Total	68,404[14]

The table below gives the total importations of cotton for the United Kingdom in the first decade of the nineteenth century, and shows, in a general way, the country of origin. It illustrates in a striking manner the growing importance of the American, and particularly of the North American, sources of supply.

	1802	1804	1806	1808	1810
American . . .	107,494	104,103	124,939	37,672	389,605
Brazil	74,720	48,588	51,034	50,442	
East India . . .	8,535	3,561	7,787	12,512	79,382
Other sorts . . .	90,634	86,358	77,978	67,512	92,186
Totals . . .	281,383	242,610	261,738	168,138	561,173[15]

[14] Smithers, *Liverpool*, p. 147.

[15] *Liverpool Mercury*, Feb. 5, 1813, p. 254. Not specified as to whether bales or bags: account in Pitkin with same totals given in bales.

Seybert, *Statistical Annals*, 1818, p. 92, note.

Pitkin gives a more complete segregation of imports of cotton for 1810 (*Statistical View*, 1816, p. 115), as follows:

	Bales
From America	240,516
Portugal and colonies	142,946
Spain and colonies	14,589
East Indies	79,382
West India Islands	33,571
Mediterranean	3,592
Ireland	6,082
Heligoland	182
Africa	22
Demerara, Berbice, Surinam, Cayenne . .	40,291
Total bales	561,173

He states that the American bales average 300 lbs., while the bales from Portugal average not more than 100 lbs., so that "during this year, therefore, from one-half to two-thirds of all the cotton imported into Great Britain, was from the U. S."

It will be noted that by 1806 about one-half of the total imports are of North American origin. In the period which followed, and in fact all during the past century, and up to the present day, we find American cotton maintaining its supremacy in the British market.[16]

American cotton would not seem to have met with particular favor among the British spinners when first introduced. According to the records of McConnel and Kennedy, a large Manchester spinning firm, American cotton appears to have gained a prominent place in their purchases, even in the nineties, although the results of using the American "Georgia" were not wholly satisfactory, as complaints were not infrequent of the yarn spun from the "yellow wool." It was said that although "Georgia" produced a stronger yarn than "Bourbon," it was only fit for weft when spun into numbers of over 120. Nevertheless, by the beginning of the nineteenth century other growths rarely appeared among the purchases of this firm.[17] Likewise the first importations of Sea Island cotton were not enthusiastically

[16] Reliable figures of the importations of cotton from various sources are difficult to secure for this period. Page (*Commerce and Industry*, vol. II, p. 145) does not give these figures until the year 1840. The following table, however, serves to illustrate the growing importance of American cotton in the British market. It is derived from a table by Ellison (*Cotton Trade*, p. 86), and gives, for five-year periods, the average importations from various sources in percentages. The sources of his figures are not stated, and they are therefore open to some doubt, but in the main the totals for the later years agree with those given by Page (p. 140):

	United States %	Brazil %	British W. I. %	Mediterranean %	East Indies, etc. %	Sundries %	Total %
1786-1790	0.16	7.87	70.75	20.44	0.78	...	100
1796-1800	24.08	11.43	35.23	18.47	8.90	1.89	100
1806-1810	53.14	16.07	16.23	1.28	12.79	0.49	100
1816-1820	47.31	15.86	6.77	0.29	26.65	3.12	100
1826-1830	74.50	10.45	2.23	2.76	9.57	0.49	100
1836-1840	79.91	4.54	0.31	1.68	12.67	0.89	100
1846-1850	81.13	3.76	0.12	2.04	12.76	0.19	100

[17] Daniels, G. W., "American Cotton Trade under the Embargo," *Am. Hist. Review*, vol. XXI, 1916, p. 276.

The above study, and others, are partially based on the records of a Manchester spinning firm—McConnel and Kennedy. An unbroken series of these records from 1795-1835 enables Mr. Daniels to describe, with convincing emphasis, some of the details of the cotton trade. For a more complete account of these records see the introduction to Daniels' *The Early English Cotton Industry.*

welcomed. The staple was objected to as too long, and it is said that, by one or two spinners, it was literally cut shorter before it was used.[18]

The chief objection was, doubtless, that it was new to the manufacturers, and they did not know how to use it to best advantage. Certainly the increase in the consumption testifies to the growing favor which was accorded the American cotton.

THE ORGANISATION OF THE COTTON TRADE

It is but natural to expect to find the organisation for the handling of cotton a relatively simple one in the early period, and particularly so in the years before 1800. Unfortunately, evidence does not seem to be available to enable one to give in precise detail the agencies then existing and the methods which they pursued in carrying on their business. One would also expect, with the increase in the volume of business, to find new agencies arising, old forms of organisation proving themselves to be unfit to carry on the work, and dying out; other units expanding in importance to meet new needs and conditions.

The period from 1800 to 1850 was, broadly speaking, one in which the utility of the different agencies in the cotton trade was tested out; and during that period we have the beginnings of the modern organisation of the trade—although the most modern and most revolutionary feature, the development of a market in cotton futures, did not come about until after the close of the period we are studying. But it was a period in which there was a development from a relatively simple, undifferentiated organisation, to one that was highly complex and specialised, especially adapted to meet the needs of the trade in cotton.

THE IMPORTING HOUSES

Our earliest sources on the nature of the houses importing cotton would lead us to believe them to have been, principally, commission agents or factors. This means, of course, that the cotton was not purchased outright by a British firm, but was consigned to the British firm at the risk of, and for the account of the American exporter, whether a commercial house or a

[18] Smithers, *Liverpool*, 1825, p. 135.

Southern planter. Ellison, writing in 1886 of his memories of the cotton trade, stated that "in former years the imports were chiefly received on consignment by merchants."[19]

Schulze-Gaevernitz says of the early cotton market:

"Here, on the one hand, stood the importing merchant with his office in Liverpool. His task was to make himself conversant with the American market—a risk of such greatness, with the difficult traffic and communication conditions of the time, that he at first even imported the cotton, not at his own risk, but on commission for the account of the American, against cash on account."[20]

An American writer in 1820 showed the importance of consignment on American account when he stated that:

"From December, 1818, to April, 1819, the productions of the United States fell in Liverpool, upon an average, one-third in their price. Cotton fell much more. Nearly the whole of this loss was sustained by the merchants of this country."[21]

The committee, in its report of 1823, indicated, by implication at least, that most of the cotton was received on consignment, for it stated that the usual course of proceeding in Liverpool appeared to be for the importers, *"acting as the apparent owners,"* to apply to the brokers for advances.[22] Another witness before the same Parliamentary Committee said that "a large proportion [of the cotton] is on the account of American owners and other foreign merchants; but a great deal comes on account of manufacturers in this country."[23]

It does not seem unreasonable to assume that most of the importing houses were commission houses. We have already seen

[19] Ellison, *Cotton Trade,* 1886, p. 279. Ellison gives the most complete account of the early cotton trade found anywhere. He was engaged in business, apparently successfully, as a cotton broker. Much of his information must be first hand; some of it probably traditional. In general his statements have checked with other sources. Where Ellison is quoted as the sole authority, the reader is advised that the statements are given only as tentative conclusions.

[20] Schulze-Gaevernitz, G. von, 1895, *Cotton Trade in England,* p. 55. No authority is cited in support of this statement.

[21] *Trade and Commerce of New York,* 1820, p. 34.

[22] Parl. Papers, Report on Law Relating to Merchants, 1823, IV (452), p. 14. (Italics inserted.)

[23] *Ibid.,* p. 110.

that in many branches of foreign trade in Great Britain, it was the custom for the importers to act as factors in the sale of the produce.[24] In fact, the position of the factor was of such importance that we find a special parliamentary inquiry in 1823 devoted to the question of his legal and economic status. Again, the risks of importing, referred to by Schulze-Gaevernitz, were real risks. The possibilities of American cotton culture were by no means exhausted, the demand of the British spinner was still in a formative state, and the political state of Europe none too favorable, particularly during the Napoleonic Wars, for the assumption of unnecessary risks.

The importing commission merchant, at least in the earlier period, generally, was not confined to the handling of cotton alone. One of the largest importers of American produce mentioned tobacco and cotton as forming his principal imports.[25] Another mercantile firm, John Gore and Company, confessed to importing "every article almost," and specified cotton, silk, sugar, and coffee.[26] It is believed that it was generally customary for the commission merchant to handle other articles in addition to cotton.

It would be, however, a grave error to assume that all the cotton was imported by commission merchants acting on behalf of others. In fact, the general tendency during this half-century seems to have been for the merchant who imported on his own account to become more and more important. Possibly the beginning of importing on one's own account may be found in a desire to speculate—to assume fairly large risks for the chance of making large gains. But it seems to me that the explanation probably rests on a twofold foundation. First, with the close of the Napoleonic Wars the trade with America could be carried on with much less risk, the importing merchants had gained experience in handling a larger volume of business, and could foresee the probabilities more surely than earlier. In the second place, the increasing capital resources of the merchants made it possible for them to purchase outright, and the increasing competition among themselves made it necessary to do so. Ellison tells us that competition amongst the importers reduced the rate

[24] *Vide* Chapter II, pp. 10 ff.
[25] Parl. Papers, Evidence on Petitions of Merchants, 1808 (119), p. 33.
[26] Parl. Papers, Report on Law Relating to Merchants, 1823, p. 138.

of commission charged for the commission business.[27] Buying outright seems a development along the same line.

In the beginning a particular firm might both buy cotton on its own account, and receive cotton on commission. The Parliamentary Committee in its report of 1823 said in reference to the cotton trade:

"The witnesses state, that . . . there are few merchants who are not factors, and few factors who are not also merchants."[28]

That it was becoming more common for the cotton to be imported into Great Britain on the account of the British importer is indicated as early as 1812. In an inquiry by Parliament into the effects of the Orders in Council, Mr. Thornely stated that he believed that a considerable proportion of the exports from the United States were on British account. When asked his reasons, he replied:

"Because I know that houses in Manchester send agents to America, to purchase cotton in Charlestown, and that English houses, many of them, have agents in America, and that they do business on their own account, whenever it appears likely to answer their purpose."[29]

A mercantile house in Liverpool, called 'C. and D.' in the report, was apparently in the habit of dealing on its own account, for when it deposited a cargo of cotton with a broker for sale, it had no difficulty in securing an advance, on the statement that the cotton was its property. It developed, however, that in this particular instance, the firm was acting as a commission agent for a factor in the United States.[30]

Mr. Gabriel Shaw, of the firm of Thomas Wilson and Company, handled silk, wool, and cotton on a commission basis. He stated, in 1833, that the firm did business on its own account, but apparently the commission business was the more important.[31] Mr. Ewart, a commission merchant and broker, was asked, when he appeared before the committee that examined Shaw, as to whether the American produce was imported into Liverpool chiefly on American or British account. He replied that a great deal was imported on American and on British ac-

27 Ellison, *Cotton Trade*, 1886, p. 279.
28 Parl. Papers, Report on Law Relating to Merchants, 1823, p. 14.
29 Parl. Papers, Report on Orders in Council, 1812 (210), p. 355.
30 Parl. Papers, Report on Merchants, 1823, p. 109.
31 Parl. Papers, Report on Manufactures, 1833, VI (690), p. 91, §1469.

count but that he could give no accurate estimate of the relative importance of either.[32]

With the development of the trade it became more and more the tendency for the merchants to purchase the cotton outright in America, although the consignment business still continued.

In 1833 a witness before a Parliamentary Committee was questioned on this point. In reply to the question as to whether there was a disposition to make consignments on foreign account, instead of importing on one's own account, he replied:

"I think on the contrary; the importation of goods on British account is increasing; I believe that the amount of goods exported by manufacturers for their own account is increasing, and the returns for those goods are made for their own account, and in that way the importation of foreign articles on British account is increasing."[33]

Mr. A. H. Wylie, who was principally engaged in the American trade and in the cotton importing business, gave a very definite statement in evidence in 1847. He said:

"The cotton in Liverpool is either imported on account of Merchants, residing there, or on account of the Spinner, but that which is imported on account of the Spinner generally goes direct to his Mill, and does not come into the Liverpool Market; but the great bulk is imported either on account of the Merchant in Liverpool, or on account of the Merchant or Planter in America; but this last is the smaller interest."[34]

Ellison supports Mr. Wylie in the statement that the imports on account of the American merchant or planter constituted the smaller interest. He stated that much of the cotton was purchased in America, but that this method became especially characteristic after the laying down of the Atlantic cable, so that, at the time when he was writing (1886),

"Firm offers of cotton were cabled from the other side, . . . These offers were accepted if they were at such prices as would enable the house on this side to sell 'futures' against them at a profit. . . . The old-fashioned commission merchant is out."[35]

[32] Parl. Papers, Report on Manufactures, 1833, p. 253, §§4138-4139.
[33] Parl. Papers, Report on Manufactures, 1833, p. 93.
[34] Parl. Papers, Report on Commercial Distress, 1847-1848, vol. XXIV (31), p. 228.
[35] Ellison, *op. cit.*, p. 280. Shaw testified to the profit in importing cotton when he said: "A party shipping cotton from the United States to England upon his own account, is deriving a profit of from five to ten per cent at this moment." Report on Manufactures, 1833, VI (690), p. 95.

It may be asked through what agencies the British firms purchased their cotton in the United States. The possible agencies would seem to have been either branch houses or agents of the British firms, located in America, or American commission houses or individuals acting as correspondents. It is an interesting question as to how common branch houses in the United States were, and just what they were. There seems, however, to be little indication of a definite nature, either as to their importance, or as to the nationality of the branch house, whether it was composed of Americans acting for the British, or whether composed of British sent over specifically for that purpose.

We shall see, when we come to the subject of exporting British manufactures to the United States, that it was the custom to send British agents to America to superintend the sale of the goods. Chance references indicate that branch houses or buying agents at least were not uncommon. Thornley, whose evidence has already been cited,[36] showed that in 1812 it was not uncommon for the English firms to have branches for the purpose of buying in the United States. Finley, a general merchant, gave the following account of his business:

"I am engaged in business as a general merchant in the city of London, also in the city of Glasgow, and until very lately in Liverpool. . . . I may mention also at Charlestown, in the United States, in New York, and at New Orleans; but all these latter four businesses have, within these few months, been discontinued."[37]

Mr. Wylie, a part of whose evidence has been quoted above, mentioned the fact that his house had a branch house at New Orleans, and further stated, in response to questioning on the subject, that most of the houses in Liverpool "are connected with such houses [corresponding houses] directly or indirectly." It is probable that the indirect connection would be through commission agents in the United States who would purchase cotton in the open market for shipment to Great Britain on a regular commission basis, upon the receipt of orders to that effect.[38]

The duties of a commission merchant with respect to the handling of cotton were numerous and varied. He had to see the

[36] Vide p. 40.

[37] Parl. Papers, Report on Manufactures. 1833, p. 35.

[38] Parl. Papers, Report on Commercial Distress, 1847-1848, vol. XXIV (31), p. 228, §1957.

cotton through the customs; have it stored in a place so that it might be properly viewed; pay the freight from America and the insurance premiums, in many cases; and, finally, see to the selling, either by selling it himself, or by placing it in the proper hands for disposal. For these services he charged at first a commission of two and one-half per cent. Ellison stated that competition for consignments reduced this commission to one and one-half per cent.[39] Of course the actual costs incurred, as well as the commission charged, were debited to the account of the consignor.

But his function did not end in the mere handling of the consignment. He filled an important rôle besides, in the granting of credit. In general, it may be said that it was the invariable custom for a commission house to advance funds to the American exporter. The subject has already been treated in the chapter on the agencies of trade, but in order to emphasize the point, the following testimony is submitted:

"Is it usual at Liverpool for the houses of agency to advance money on account of consignments they receive? Yes.

"Is not the trade carried on in that way to a very great extent? Yes.

"As a large commission house yourself, do you believe, it would be possible for any persons to obtain consignments to any extent from the United States without making these advances? No, generally speaking, I do not think you could have consignments from the United States without making advances."[40]

Probably funds were not advanced directly, for the custom was that common in all lines of commission business, of accepting bills drawn against the firm. These bills could be discounted in the American market, giving to the exporter the control of immediate funds. It was not usual for the exporter to draw a bill for the full face value of the invoice, but for from two-thirds to three-fourths of the face value. The amount apparently varied with the times and the nature of the relationship of the exporter and his agent in Liverpool.[41]

[39] Ellison, *Cotton Trade*, 1886, p. 279.

[40] Parl. Papers, Report on Manufactures, 1833, p. 253.

[41] Parl. Papers, Report on Merchants, pp. 49, 55, 109. Hunt, *Merchants' Magazine*, 1840, II, p. 336.

In this connection attention is called to a letter from a Savannah commission merchant in 1815, quoted on page 63. It will be noted that the custom was for the importing house to name a Northern house on whom the commission agent in the Southern market might draw his bills.

The Liverpool house must obviously have kept open accounts with any American exporter with whom it did a regular business. The account could not be closed until the sale had been effected, and an account rendered. In the meantime possibly another cargo had been shipped, and so on. In 1833 a merchant of Georgia shipped two hundred bales of cotton consigned to William and James Brown and Company of Liverpool, invoiced at $9,151.77. On shipment he drew a draft on the house of Brown Brothers and Company of New York (composed either wholly or partly of partners of the Liverpool house) for $9,000. It was explained that the reason that the draft was so near the face value of the invoice was because he was owed sums from previous shipments.[42]

When cotton was purchased outright by the branch house or an agent, it was a cash transaction. Quoting Mr. Wylie again:

"If, for instance, my house in New Orleans purchased Cotton there for shipment to me in Liverpool, they would have to pay cash for it to the planter or to his Agent, and we of course would be out of funds until either the Cotton was sold, or we obtained funds by some other means; but generally speaking, until the cotton was sold."

And further:

"Then as between Importer and the Merchant in the Cotton State, it is a Ready Money Transaction? A Cash transaction, and almost always before delivery."[43]

Another point remains to be noticed, and that concerns the activities of the commission house or the importing house as exporting agents, particularly of British manufacturers. Among the numbers of merchants called before the Parliamentary Committees in the first half of the nineteenth century, there appear to have been few, if any, who were engaged solely in the business of importing cotton. A few instances, among many possible examples, may be cited. The firm of William and John Bell and Company (1808) were "in the habit of exporting goods, generally of the manufactures of this country, to America, and receiving consignments here," principally of tobacco and cotton, "also remittances from the continent of bills which are occasion-

42 Hunt, *Merchants' Magazine*, 1840, II, p. 336.
43 Parl. Papers, Report on Commercial Distress, 1847-1848, XXIV (31), p. 229, §§1966-1967.

ally drawn upon houses from America."[44] The firm of Martin, Hope and Thornely (1812) were merchants engaged largely in the American trade, and carried on a business similar to that of the firm just mentioned.[45] John Wily (1818), a merchant engaged in the export of manufactured goods, specifically cotton goods, was also an importer of coffee, sugar, and cotton.[46] The house of Baring Brothers and Company (1833) called itself "Import and Export Commission Merchants," and dealt largely with the United States.[47] Mr. Wylie (1847) was an exporter of manufactured goods to the United States, as well as an importer of cotton. In fact, he stated that "the importers of raw materials are generally exporters of Manufactured Goods."[48]

THE DEALERS

It might seem that the simplest method of procedure was for the spinner to go directly to a merchant or commission merchant and buy the cotton he needed. That this was done is doubtless true, but there is no evidence to show that it was ever characteristic or typical of the cotton trade. Instead we find various middlemen intervening between the importer and the manufacturer. In the earlier period, and particularly until about 1810, there was a class of business men known as "dealers" predominant in the trade.

The first evidence of the presence of the dealer which has appeared is given in an early report on the linen trade. Tipping, a linen manufacturer, in 1751 thus described, if not the dealer of 1800, at least his prototype:

"There are people both at London and Manchester who have bought up great Quantities [of cotton], and sold them in Course; but he never saw any Person buy Cotton and after refuse to sell it. They sold it to the Manufacturers; . . . But he knows several Persons, who have made it their business to go to Liverpoole and Lancaster to buy Cotton, which they have sold out immediately to the Manufacturers at a very small profit, though dearer every week; and have gone to Liverpoole every

44 Parl. Papers, Evidence on Petitions of Merchants, 1808 (119), p. 33.
45 Parl. Papers, Report on Orders in Council, 1812 (310), p. 355.
46 Parl. Papers, Report on Duties on Cotton Prints, 1818, III (279), p. 26.
47 Parl. Papers, Report on Manufactures, 1833, pp. 45, 57.
48 Parl. Papers, Report on Commercial Distress, 1847-1848, XXIV (31), pp. 233, 242.

week to buy it, and sell it again, and have gone the next week, and laid out the same money."[49]

This gives us our first characteristic of the dealer. He bought in wholesale quantities from the importer and retailed to the manufacturer.

That the dealer was an important figure in the first quarter of the nineteenth century, and that he was the dominant figure in the dealings between the importer and spinner seems hardly open to doubt. Mr. Daniels, in his study of the records of the firm of McConnel and Kennedy, noted above, says that until after the first decade of the nineteenth century, the common method was for purchases to be made through a dealer. The Manchester dealer bought his cotton in Liverpool, London, or Glasgow, or possibly imported it himself, and retailed it in small quantities to the spinner. Until the close of the eighteenth century the purchases were all small, ten bags being a considerable order; often only one or two bags were purchased at a time. During the early years of the next century the purchases became more voluminous, doubtless with the expansion of the business, running to fifty or sixty bags, and involving sums of £2,500 or £3,000, instead of the £250 which had been the case hitherto.[50] Schulze-Gaevernitz states that in the early part of the century, and indeed up to the opening of the railroad from Liverpool to Manchester, the spinner bought chiefly from the dealer.[51] Ellison gave a vivid picture of the extent of the dealers' operations. He stated:

"Some of the dealers were in a very large way of business, and many of them imported extensively on their own account. They were, in point of fact, merchants. Some of the firms kept up a stock of several thousand bales of various growths and qualities, and the spinners made their purchases after inspecting the actual bales or bags in the warehouses at Manchester."[52]

The typical dealer is described by Mr. John Slack, a cotton broker, as one who bought a moderate quantity, and an assortment to meet the demands of his customers, such as he might sell in a week or ten days.[53]

[49] Parl. Papers, 1st Series, 1751, vol. II, p. 294, Report on Linen Trade.
[50] Daniels, G. W., "Early Records of a Great Manchester Cotton Spinning Firm," *Econ. Journal*, 1915, vol. XXV, p. 179.
[51] Schulze-Gaevernitz, *Cotton Trade*, 1892, p. 69.
[52] Ellison, *Cotton Trade*, 1886, p. 175.
[53] *Ibid.*, p. 245. Quotation cited in Ellison and attributed to John Slack,

The dealer might secure his cotton in several ways. It has already been suggested that in many cases he imported cotton,[54] but probably his chief purchases were made in the Liverpool cotton market from the specialists in importing. He might go to the importer and make a private bargain; again, he might attend one of the many public sales or auctions, and buy the cotton himself, directly, or indirectly through a cotton broker. In any case he would transport the cotton to his warehouses in Manchester, Preston, or some manufacturing centre, and there hold it until finally sold to the spinner.

It seems quite clear that the dealer must have performed economic services sufficiently important to have justified his existence. His activities not only made it unnecessary for the spinner to make the long journey to Liverpool, and allowed him to concentrate on that for which he was, presumably, best fitted, but also they allowed the importing merchant to devote his attention largely to the foreign market, by making it unnecessary for him to go out and seek his customers.

But the dealer's most important function seems to have been that of supplying the spinners with the credit necessary to expand their business. The dealer in the nineties, when McConnel and Kennedy were buying in very small amounts, usually sold on a basis of "two and two months," meaning a credit of two months and payment at the end of that time by a two months' bill. But with an increase in the quantities purchased, there was also an extension of credit. Instead of two months, we find four, and in some cases as much as eight months' credit allowed, five or six months being by no means uncommon. Daniels suggests that part of the explanation of the extension of credit is that the firm had secured the confidence of the dealers.[55] A later account of the dealer notes that he gave credit of from fourteen days to three months to the manufacturer, with payment at the end of the period, presumably by a bill.[56] When the spinner bought from the importer directly or through a broker, the terms were

Remarks on the Cotton Trade, 1816. "The regular and steady dealers are those who buy a moderate Quantity, and an assortment to meet the demands of their customers, and such as they may feasibly calculate to run off in a week or ten days, and then go to market again."

[54] *Cf.* also quotation above.

[55] Daniels, "Records," *Econ. Journal*, 1915, vol. XXV, p. 179.

[56] Parl. Papers, Report on Manufactures, 1833, VI (690), p. 559.

almost invariably a credit of ten days and payment by a three months' bill.[57] The importance of liberal credit to a business that was rapidly expanding cannot, I think, be overestimated.

But the era of the dealer did not last long. He seems to have been supreme from, say, 1810 to 1815. From 1815 on, his importance decreased, although he lingered on throughout the half century. Ellison stated that in 1815 there were more than one hundred cotton merchants or dealers in Manchester, and many more besides in the manufacturing and spinning districts.[58] Daniels noted that in the case of the firm of McConnel and Kennedy it had ceased to be customary after 1812 to purchase from the dealer, and that purchases were made directly from the importer, through the medium of the broker.[59]

The general causes of the decline in importance and numbers of the dealers will be considered in connection with the rise of the class of buying and selling brokers. Our purpose here is merely to show that a decline did take place. It should be realised, of course, that there was no sharp break, but a gradual increase in the size of the broker class, and in the volume of business which it transacted, and a gradual melting away of the class known as dealers.

A study of the business directories of the manufacturing centres, particularly of Manchester, at various dates, would be very profitable. None has been available, except that for Preston. In a directory of 1821 we note that there are five firms or individuals listed as "cotton and twist dealers." In 1842 none is given.[60]

[57] Parl. Papers, Report on Manufactures, 1833, VI (690), pp. 91, 559.

Parl. Papers, Report on Commercial Distress, 1847-1848, XXIV (31), p. 229. §1968. "As between the importing Merchant and the Manufacturer, what is the nature of the transaction? They have the option of paying at Ten Days, less the Discount; but generally the Payment is made by a Bankers' Bill at Three Months.

§1969. "Is the paying Cash for the Cotton a Course of Trade, which has been introduced within the last few years, or has it been the Case as long as you have been connected with the Trade? As long as I have known it.

§1970. "Does it apply to other Ports as well? To all the Cotton Ports, and arises from the Fact that the weighing, marking, and shipping is a tedious Process, and until this be effected the delivery can scarcely be said to be completed, but the Purchaser has a Lien on the Cotton which is at once turned over to him."

[58] Ellison, *Cotton Trade*, 1886, p. 176.

[59] Daniels, "Records," *Econ. Journal*, 1915, vol. XXV, p. 180.

[60] Whittle, P., *History of Preston*, 1821, vol. I, p. 327.

A commercial directory of Preston and its environs . . . 1842.

We find mention of the dealers all during this period, and as late as 1841. In 1826 in a cotton report published in the *Liverpool Mercury* we see that on June 30 the cotton sold on that day—2,000 bags—had been "sold chiefly amongst exporters, dealers, and speculators."[61] Again in 1833 a witness testified as follows:

"Are there any thriving merchants that buy the cotton of the importing merchants and sell it again? Yes; that trade is carried on.

"Are there any thriving merchants that carry on that business exclusively? Yes; there are many in Manchester who still go to Liverpool to buy cotton, and sell it again.

"They [the spinners] generally buy the cotton through the first hands, and not through the hands of an intermediate person? Exactly; and those who succeed in business will be found generally to do so."[62]

Another witness in the same year, before the same committee, testified that the class of middlemen intermediate between spinners and merchants was less numerous than ten years earlier.[63] Lanman, writing in 1841, of the cotton sales in Liverpool, spoke of the Manchester cotton dealers as important buyers in the market.[64]

By the time that Ellison wrote the dealer had, however, entirely disappeared, and if the term was used at all, it referred to an entirely different class.[65] And finally we have the word of a Manchester cotton spinner, testifying in 1870, before a French committee of inquiry, that he had no knowledge of any agent in the sale of cotton other than the broker.[66]

THE BROKERS

The growing importance of the brokers has been alluded to in the previous section on the "dealer," and the general nature of the business of the broker has been discussed in the chapter on the agencies of trade.[67] The purpose of this section is to examine

[61] *Liverpool Mercury*, June 30, 1826.
[62] Parl. Papers, Report on Manufactures, 1833, p. 559.
[63] *Ibid.*, p. 247.
[64] Hunt, *Merchants' Magazine*, 1841, IV, p. 221. Article by James H. Lanman.
[65] Ellison, *Cotton Trade*, 1886, p. 176.
[66] *Anglo-French Treaty of 1860:* 1870, p. 46.
[67] *Vide* Chapter II, pp. 17 ff.

more minutely the operations and functions of the broker in cotton.

The beginnings of brokerage in cotton are somewhat doubtful, but we do know that before 1800 the cotton broker played but a small rôle in the cotton business, and did not really become a vital part of the organisation until about 1815. Mr. Brooke tells us that in the period around 1775 and for several years thereafter, the merchants of Liverpool usually transacted their own business, and consequently the vocation of a broker was but little pursued in Liverpool. He said:

"For a considerable period the only houses of any note who called themselves brokers, were Mr. Thomas Ryan, Mr. James Drinkwater, Mr. Woodward, and Mr. George Dunbar."[68]

Some of these were apparently engaged in the cotton trade, for Ellison found mention of them before 1775. He wrote:

"The first brokers of whom we have any mention, engaged in the sale of cotton, were Mr. George Drinkwater . . . , who, in 1766, and a few years previously, conducted his business in Thomas Street; and Mr. Charles Lowndes, . . . Mr. Drinkwater was broker to the Underwriters, and in that capacity on the 20th September, 1766, sold a quantity of damaged cotton saved out of the 'Molly' from Granada. . . . The cotton, prior to sale, was on view at the warehouse of Mr. William Rathbone, 'at the top of South Dock.' Between 1766 and 1776 we find Mr. Thomas Ryan, of Exchange Alley; Mr. Samuel Woodward, of Oldhall Street; Mr. Joshua Holt, with a house in Moor Street, and a warehouse in Old Roperty."[69]

Ellison suggested as the reason for the small number of brokers the fact that in 1770 only 6,000 bags were sold, and that much of that was sold directly to the dealers. Consequently there could have been little need for the services of a broker.[70]

These brokers were not, at least in origin, confined to the selling or buying of cotton, but apparently handled any article which might be entrusted to them. In all probability a given broker might be more conversant with one line of goods—for example, West India goods—than with another, and the major portion of his business would be in that line. Ellison stated that, with the exception of Mr. Holt, all of the brokers whom

68 Brooke, *Liverpool*, 1853, p. 232.
69 Ellison, *Cotton Trade*, 1886, p. 166.
70 Ellison, *Cotton Trade*, 1886, p. 166.

he mentioned were general brokers. Holt was exclusively a buying broker of cotton, but it is significant that, in the beginning buying cotton was merely incidental to his business as a stay-maker, which he pursued in Manchester.

With the increased volume of business to be handled, some of the brokers, including Mr. Holt, abandoned their other lines, and became cotton brokers only.[71] This, however, seems to have been a very gradual process. A study of the advertisements of auction sales by brokers in Liverpool for the period July 7 to December 29, 1826, shows out of fifteen brokerage firms advertising sales, there were only four which advertised sales of cotton only. For example, at different times during this period, Yates Brothers advertised for public sale cotton, indigo, coffee, sugar, logwood, cocoa, a ship; Duff Finley and Company, ox-hides, horns, coffee, sugar, flour, fustic, gum arabic, valonia, lumber, cotton; Joseph McViccar, cotton, tablecloths and napkins, flour, turpentine, harness, shoes, American apples, hides, lumber; and many other examples might be given. It will be noted that in most cases the commodities offered for sale by a particular broker seem to have been, in general, goods from a particular region—thus the goods advertised by Yates Brothers might well have been picked up by a ship in the India trade.[72]

Two types of brokers appear, the buying broker, representing the interests of the spinner or dealer, and the selling broker, the representative of the importing merchant. At the outset the two classes of brokers were not clearly differentiated, although most of the brokers were selling brokers. Mr. Holt, as mentioned above, was the first exclusively buying broker. But by 1810 there

[71] Ellison, *Cotton Trade*, 1886, p. 167.
''All these dealt in other articles besides cotton; and as yet Mr. Joshua Holt was the only cotton broker properly so-called. He was also the only exclusively buying broker, the others being exclusively selling brokers, with the exception of Mr. Charles Lowndes, who occasionally bought for dealers. Mr. Holt's business as a stay-maker had brought him into contact with several Manchester people, on whose account he was commissioned to examine and report upon the West India cotton imported into Liverpool, and for which purpose he was in the habit of interviewing importers and visiting warehouses in which such cotton was stored on landing. He had acquired a special technical knowledge of the staple of cotton, and for the most part had always orders in hand to purchase any lots of fine or long staple that might be offered for sale, and for which he was paid so much per pound for his trouble.''
[72] *Liverpool Mercury*, July 9-December 29, 1826.

were brokers who sold or bought only, as well as others who both bought and sold. It is impossible to determine which was really typical—the exclusively buying or selling broker, or the broker who both bought and sold. Ellison would lead us to believe that the former was the more usual.[73] On the other hand, we have contemporary evidence to show that the broker who both bought and sold was, as late as 1841, the characteristic figure in the market. An anonymous cotton spinner said of the Liverpool brokerage system:

"The bane of that system is, that, with few exceptions, every broker is at once a buyer and a seller of cotton. He therefore stands in an anomalous position. He is in the pay of two parties, whose interests and objects are diametrically opposed, and whose interests therefore he cannot equally and simultaneously serve."[74]

It is a question which, it must be confessed, cannot be solved with the information available. It is true that Ellison wrote considerably after the period which we are discussing, and may therefore have tended to read into the past the customs of his time. But it is equally obvious that the anonymous spinner was not at all pleased with the Liverpool brokerage system, for the underlying motive of his exposé of the system was to show that there was no necessity for the buying broker. In this connection he remarked:

"If the present system is to remain intact, the severe sufferings of the members of the Cotton Trade will lead them to ask, of what use are buying brokers at all?"[75]

While therefore the ultimate solution of this question must remain a problem of the future, it does appear unquestionable that the brokers were a most vital part of the organisation. Other testimony bears out this statement. Smithers stated in 1825 that there "are now about ninety houses engaged as cotton brokers at Liverpool."[76] Samuel Hope, in 1823, testified that he had been in business as a cotton broker for twenty-one years, and his evidence gives the impression that his was a normal line of busi-

---

[73] Ellison, *Cotton Trade*, 1886, p. 273.
[74] *Anomalies of the Cotton Trade*, 1841, p. 10.
[75] *Anomalies of the Cotton Trade*, 1841, pp. 19-20.
[76] Smithers, *Liverpool*, 1825, p. 140.

ness.[77] Baines indicated the existence of the two classes of brokers, and said that "the buyers, who are the Manchester cotton dealers [showing the persistence of that class], and the spinners all over the country, also employ brokers . . . to make their purchases."[78] Finally, the evidence given before the Committee to Investigate Commercial Distress in 1847-1848 shows that in that period the common method of selling cotton was through a broker.[79]

The rise of the selling broker presents, it seems to me, little difficulty. It has been shown that selling brokers were a normal part of the trade organisation, and had existed in the cotton trade from a fairly early time. With the expansion of the business, and with the growing complexity of trade relations, we should naturally expect to find them more numerous.

The rise of the buying broker, on the other hand, is clearly connected with the decline in the numbers and importance of the dealers. In many cases the dealers themselves found it desirable to employ agents to purchase their cotton for them, and probably many of the buying brokers started in business in this way. But many of them began in business as buying agents for a spinning firm, or a group of spinning firms, who felt themselves in a position to ignore the dealer and negotiate directly with the importer. It is not an unreasonable theory to connect the fall of the dealer with the increasing self-sufficiency of the spinners. It has already been noted that the dealer gave credit of several months longer than the importer was willing to give. It seems hardly open to doubt that a firm purchasing cotton on the short credit basis would be able to secure better prices. With expanded resources, many of the spinning firms were able to take advantage of this saving. On the other hand, many of the smaller firms were not, and we have the dealer still lingering on well towards 1850.

Of the activity of the spinners in securing agents to purchase cotton for them directly, Ellison remarked:

[77] Parl. Papers, Report on Merchants, 1823, p. 153.

It is interesting to note that in the list of brokerage firms advertising auction sales in Liverpool during the six months period mentioned above, Samuel Hope and Company was one of the four firms that advertised sales of cotton only.

[78] Baines, *Cotton Manufacture*, 1835, p. 318.

[79] Parl. Papers, Report on Commercial Distress, 1847-1848, XXIV (31), pp. 228, 266.

"The movement [after 1810] was strongly opposed by the dealers, who, shortly after a number of spinners had set up several brokers to represent them in Liverpool, held a meeting in Manchester, and resolved neither to buy from, nor to deal with, any broker in Liverpool who sold to the newly-established buying houses. But this opposition melted away before the determination of the spinners to retain the advantages which they had gained by buying in the larger market, where sellers were more numerous, and the competition more open, than was the case in Manchester."[80]

The new brokers were in many cases friends or relatives of the spinners, and in some cases were dealers who had found their business unprofitable. Daniels tells us that by 1812 the firm had ceased to buy from dealers, and made their purchases exclusively through brokers. He notes that in many instances the buying brokers were the same houses or persons from whom, as dealers, the firm had previously purchased their cotton. This suggests that the rise of the broker and the decline of the dealer may have meant, in not a few instances, merely a change of function.[81]

The usual business of the broker was simply that of an agent who transacted business at the order of, and for the account of a principal, having himself no interest in the transaction other than making a purchase or effecting a sale.[82] For this service he received a commission. At first a commission of one per cent was paid the selling brokers, and from ½d. to 1d. per pound paid to the buying broker. Competition, and improvements in the methods of carrying on the business, resulting in a lessening of the amount of work required to make purchases and sales, reduced the commission for both buying and selling brokers to one-half of one per cent.[83]

But while this was the normal business of the broker, it must be remembered that business was in a process of transition, and probably few of the actual firms conformed at all times during

[80] Ellison, *Cotton Trade*, 1886, p. 176.
[81] Daniels, *Econ. Journal*, XXV, pp. 179, 180.
[82] Parl. Papers, Report on Commercial Distress, 1847-1848, XXIV (31), p. 228.
[83] Ellison, *Cotton Trade*, 1886, pp. 166, 175.
Smithers, *Liverpool*, 1825, p. 140.
Baines, *Cotton Manufacture*, 1835, p. 318.
Parl. Papers, Report on Commercial Distress, 1847-1848, XXIV (31), p. 228.

their career to the type described. Mr. Hope, who has been cited
as an example of a cotton broker, specialising solely in cotton,
did not conform in other respects, for he confessed to have imported occasionally on his own account, and "(as is almost universally the case) received also consignments from abroad."[84]
The abuse, for so it was regarded in some quarters, of dealing
on one's own account and at the same time acting as a broker
for others, engaged the attention of John Slack in 1816, who
complained:

"A great evil exists both in London and Liverpool, by brokers being both merchants and dealers; the duty, and only duty of a broker
is to be a middleman between the buyer and seller, and not to buy and
sell on his own account."[85]

But whether or not an abuse, this practice continued and
grew to be of greater importance later in the nineteenth century,
until we find little difference between the importer and the
broker.

Another service performed by the broker was the furnishing
of credit facilities to the importer. In spite of the short term on
which cotton was sold, it seems to have been necessary for the
importer to seek assistance outside his own business. The broker
appears to have been the natural agent for this, and we find it
customary for the importer, early in the nineteenth century, to
draw bills of exchange on the broker as soon as the cotton was
placed in the broker's hands for sale. The broker would accept
the bills, and the merchant could then get these bills discounted
by the banks, who considered them first-class paper.[86] The following account indicates to what an extent the brokers might be
called upon for advances:

"Every man of business knows that when goods are sent for sale to
this country, the consignor draws in general, at two or three months
date, upon the consignee (at the time when he transmits bills of lading) for two thirds or three fourths of their value; these bills frequently fall due before advantageous sales can be made of the goods,
or when the goods are sold, but the funds not received the merchant
then, if his stock of goods be large, and his own funds locked up, ap-

84 Parl. Papers, Report on Merchants, 1823, p. 153.

85 Quoted in Ellison, *Cotton Trade*, 1886, p. 244.

86 Parl. Papers, Report on Merchants, 1823, pp. 53, 153. Testimony of
Samuel Hope and Joseph Trueman, both brokers.

plies to his broker for a sum of money on account of the sales, or to his banker, who will advance on the brokers' bill or engagement to pay the same out of the proceeds as they are received."[87]

By 1847-1848 it was a well-recognised custom, to the prevalence of which a number of witnesses testified. One witness stated that

". . . the Quantity of cotton which has come to Liverpool at various times is so great that without accommodations of that kind on the part of the brokers to the merchant, or by the banker to the holders of cotton, it would be impossible to hold that stock which is necessary for the consumption of the country."[88]

It was a device which might, apparently, encourage speculation as well as legitimate business, for it was stated that many people who had no capital of their own, had been able to make speculative purchases by drawing extensively upon the cotton brokers. It was estimated that they had drawn bills on one broker up to £500,000 or £600,000, but this speculative business was confined to a few brokers only.[89]

The relations existing between the broker and his principal were friendly and enduring. No merchant attempted to deal directly with a buying broker; had he done so, he would have been referred to his selling broker. Nor did the buying broker attempt to deal directly with the importing merchant. It was against the etiquette of the market for any broker, buying or selling, to poach upon the ground of any fellow broker. Individual importing firms frequently employed more than one broker—it was not possible for the larger merchants to do otherwise; but individual spinning firms rarely employed more than one broker, and to this broker they remained, as a rule, firmly attached. The new firms of brokers which were founded by the direct assistance of the merchants or the spinners found a ready welcome from the old brokers. The result of this general good feeling was a spirit of universal trustfulness; all transactions were plain and aboveboard, there was no secrecy; every broker who cared to know, could know what his fellow brokers were

[87] Parl. Papers, Report on Merchants, 1823, p. 113.

[88] Parl. Papers, Report on Commercial Distress, 1847-1848, XXIV (31), p. 266.

[89] Parl. Papers, Report on Commercial Distress, 1847-1848, XXVII (213), p. 43.

doing. There was no wrangling between merchants and brokers on the one hand, nor between spinners and brokers on the other.[90]

METHODS OF SALE

Sale by Auction. The sale of goods by auction has been, and still is, of importance in various markets. In many cases it is resorted to as a means of disposing of odd lots, damaged goods, or goods difficult to classify. In other cases, as in the trade in wool, it holds a much more important position, and is a regular part of the organisation.

In the cotton trade sales by auction have not been without their importance, and in the early period were particularly important. Below are given two samples of advertisements appearing in a Liverpool newspaper in 1784. It will be noted that the amounts seem small, but compared with the total imports in that year they loom up as fairly significant.

"To be sold by auction at George's Coffee House, on April 15th, 1784, at eleven in the forenoon, 133 bags and 278 pockets of fine St. Domingo cotton. The cotton lies in Mr. Blundell's warehouse, Covent Garden, where it may be viewed, and samples will be laid out in the salesroom the day before the sale. George Dunbar, broker."

"To be sold, at the office of Thomas Ryan, in Exchange Alley, on April 14, 1784 (sale to begin at eleven o'clock), for the purpose of settling a dispute respecting the same, 44 bags of Grenada cotton, 25 bags of Demerary, 18 bags St. Domingo, 50 serons Spanish, and 25 bags damaged. Thomas Ryan, broker."[91]

The sales of cotton by auction do not seem in this period to have been merely occasional odd lots, for we find mention of such sales during the entire first quarter of the nineteenth century.

A search for advertisements of cotton auctions in the *Liverpool Mercury* in the year 1811 revealed very few advertise-

---

[90] Ellison, *Cotton Trade*, 1886, p. 273.
It was, however, possible, and in many cases customary, for the spinner to deal directly with the selling broker without the mediation of the buying broker. *Cf. Anomalies of the Cotton Trade*, 1841, p. 20. But apparently the trend was in the direction of absolute dependence of the spinner on the broker. *Cf.* the statement of the Manchester manufacturer in 1870 that whether the spinner assisted the broker in his selection of the cotton or not, the brokerage was the same. *Anglo-French Treaty of 1860:* 1870, p. 46.

[91] Quoted in Ellison, *Cotton Trade*, 1886, pp. 167-168, from *Williamson's Advertiser.*

ments of any sort, and particularly few of cotton. A similar search in the year 1820 gave evidence of the universality of the practice. The most respectable firms advertised cotton of practically all descriptions. On September 15, 1820, there were over 9,000 bales of cotton advertised for sale at auction by six firms of brokers. Most of the cotton was American cotton, but there were a few bales of Indian and Bourbon. One firm, that of Samuel Hope and Company, offered a total of 3,270 bales of New Orleans and Alabama cotton.[92]

In the period from the 7th of July to the 29th of December, 1820, thirty-four advertisements of auction sales in cotton were found. On September 22 of the same year (a week after the sales above were advertised, and hence presumably speaking of the sale of the goods advertised) the *Mercury* remarked that "the quantity of cotton offered for public sale here on Friday last is said to exceed that which has been offered on any other day since the rise of this port."[93] In 1825 we have evidence of probably one of the largest auctions ever held, for it was noted that the usual salesrooms were not large enough to hold the assembled company. There were offered for sale 16,326 bags, of which 5,000 later were withdrawn, and 11,112 bales actually sold. The same report gives the figures for the private sales of the week as only 2,070 bags.[94]

But the auction method did not last. Probably the reports of the cotton market by the newspapers are not altogether trustworthy, but they are at least an indication. During 1826 the *Liverpool Mercury* gave weekly reports of the cotton market, stating the total sales during the week. It mentioned in only eight reports sales of cotton by auction. The largest number of bales sold by auction in any one week was 2,000 bales. The total sales for that week were 10,000 bales. In 1830 auction sales were mentioned only four times. The most important sale was given under the date of December 9, when 3,084 bales out of a total of 16,000 bags were sold.[95] In 1835 seven sales by auction were noted. In two other cases cotton was offered for sale at auction, but then withdrawn. The largest amount sold at auction on any

[92] *Liverpool Mercury*, July 7 to December 29, 1820.

[93] *Ibid.*, September 22, 1820.

[94] *Ibid.*, August 5, 1825. *Cf.* note on meaning of terms *bags* and *bales*, p. 31.

[95] *Ibid.*, December 9, 1830.

day in this year was 2,230 bales, out of a total of 23,170 bales sold on the same day.[96]

Furthermore, an examination of the advertisements seems to show that the cotton which was offered for sale after 1830 was in most cases not the same type of cotton which was regularly sold in the Liverpool market. In many cases it was cotton which had been damaged in some way, and in some cases it seems to have been cotton for which the demand was uncertain—as particular grades of Indian cotton.

The auction sales were in the hands of the brokers. All of the advertisements appeared over the name of some broker. Doubtless the broker might have imported cotton himself and taken charge of his own sale, but probably in most cases he was acting for some other house. The buyers were principally the buying brokers, acting as agents for spinners and dealers, or buying on their own account on speculation. In some cases we find the spinners and dealers themselves attending the auctions, although there is no evidence to show whether they bought in person and thereby evaded the brokerage charges.[97]

Private Sales of Cotton. While the sale of cotton by auction was at times an important mode of getting it into the hands of the consumer, it was not the characteristic method in use, except possibly at the beginning. Rather do we find that private bargaining, or, as it was sometimes phrased, "sales by private treaty," took the lead. When the dealer was the dominant figure in the buying world, he would get in touch with the importer or the selling broker, and personally make his purchases, or he might employ the services of a buying broker. Later we find the business almost exclusively in the hands of the buying and selling brokers.[98]

The cotton was stored in the warehouses of the various importers, where it might be viewed by anyone who had any thought of purchasing. This was an extremely wasteful and time-consuming method of transacting business. It meant that the

[96] *Liverpool Mercury*, March 14, 1835.
[97] *Liverpool Mercury*, August 5, 1825.
Smithers, *Liverpool*, 1825, p. 140.
Anglo-French Treaty of 1860: 1870, p. 46. "We would add that whether the broker selects the cotton for us, or whether the spinner assists in the selection, it is all the same, the rate of charge is one-half of one per cent."
[98] *Cf.* pp. 49 ff.

buyer would be forced personally to make the rounds of the different warehouses, inspect the actual bales, and after having compared the lots, as to quality and price, make his selection from those bales which he thought would best meet his own needs or the needs of his clients.

It seems difficult to believe that this method could have persisted for any length of time, but apparently it did. Possibly the early careless method of packing and grading followed in the United States made necessary an examination of the cotton in bulk, rather than by sample. It would be hazardous, of course, for a spinner who required cotton of an even grade to purchase a hundred bales of cotton by sample, when there might be several grades in each bale. The extra time and expense involved in the personal inspection of each bale must have been worth while in view of the losses consequent on the purchase of unsuitable cotton—losses caused by throwing men and machinery out of employment while the proper grade of cotton was being secured.

Apparently with more careful packing, which must have resulted from greater skill in handling, and a greater volume to handle, there was developed the system of selling by sample. Samples were sent to the various selling brokers' offices, where they might be viewed by the buying brokers interested. This implied a spirit of mutual confidence—confidence resting on the ability and willingness of the particular broker or importer concerned to see to it that if he sold cotton as "good New Orleans" it was good New Orleans.

This innovation of selling by sample, first proposed by a broker, was instituted some time in the first quarter of the nineteenth century. It was at the outset resisted by the majority of the brokers, who could see in it only a device to bring the buyer and seller directly together, and to eliminate the broker. It did not, however, affect their interests at all. They were able to do their work better and more efficiently, and to handle a much greater volume of cotton. In spite of the fact that the rate of brokerage dropped from one per cent to one-half of one per cent, the increased business more than compensated for the smaller remuneration.[99]

A variation of this practice of selling by sample came in later.

[99] Ellison, *Cotton Trade*, 1886, p. 175.
Baines, *Cotton Manufacture*, 1835, p. 318.

This consisted of having samples sent to the place of business of the buying broker for his inspection before he made the purchases. This had the advantage of allowing the buying brokers to compare the various samples from the different brokers at the same time, or with previous samples from the same or other brokers which they might be desirous of matching. It also enabled the spinner and the broker to examine the samples under the most favorable conditions of light, and away from the scrutiny of competing buyers.

This system was, however, never satisfactory to the selling brokers, who complained that it impeded sales. The buying brokers were alleged to have kept the samples for several hours, and thus prevented other buying brokers from securing what they might desire; they were also charged with handling them so carelessly that it was often necessary to resample. There was, therefore, a concerted move to put a stop to the practice, and on the 15th of January, 1845, a meeting was held, where it was resolved:

"That in the opinion of this meeting the practice of allowing samples of cotton to be taken from the selling brokers' office previous to sale is attended with great loss and inconvenience; and that, with the view to remedy this evil, it is proposed that the importers of cotton in this port should enter into a general resolution to instruct their selling brokers not to permit samples placed in their hands to be removed from their office until after a sale has been effected, so that all parties may have equal opportunities of inspecting them."[100]

The practical impossibility of reverting to the old methods, and the convenience of the new, made it impossible to carry this resolution into practical effect. A compromise was therefore adopted on the 28th of January:

"That of every parcel of cotton on sale, duplicate samples shall be drawn: That one set of the samples (to be distinguished by a red ticket and to be called the office sample) shall always be retained in the office of the selling broker, so as to enable the seller to exhibit his cotton to all buyers, and to give the opportunity to any buyer at once to purchase the parcel."[101]

This resolution, too, became a dead letter, and the system described above remained in force.

[100] Ellison, *Cotton Trade*, 1886, p. 177.
[101] *Ibid.*, p. 178.

In order that a large volume of business may be effectively handled, there must be a spirit of coöperation between the different agents engaged in the trade. If in all dealings it is necessary to have formal papers signed and many exchanges of memoranda, it slows down the efficiency of the organisation to a marked degree. We find striking testimony to the presence of mutual trustfulness, particularly on the part of the merchant and the broker.

The following account, paraphrased and condensed from a report of a suit at law, indicates at the same time the nature of the operations of the buying and selling brokers, and the informality of their relations. In 1840 a Mr. Bower, of the Liverpool firm of Bower and Sons, Cotton Brokers, was acting as the buying broker of a certain spinner in Lancashire. He met Mr. Earle, of the brokerage firm of Salisbury, Turner, and Earle, and inquired if he had any good Orleans cotton. It appeared that Mr. Earle had some which he was selling for a Liverpool importing firm. Both men stepped over to the office of Mr. Earle, where they examined the samples. Mr. Bower then said, "If you send these samples across to my place of business, I shall examine them, and in the course of an hour you shall have my answer." The samples were sent over, appeared to be satisfactory, a bargain was made, and the cotton invoiced. The invoice contained nothing respecting the quality of the cotton, simply the amount and the price. Throughout this transaction there was an utter absence of any form of written contract. The buying broker did not even try to take fresh samples from the bales he was buying, but merely sent a clerk over to the warehouse to see that the samples in the hands of the buying broker were samples taken from the goods in the warehouse.[102]

Baines in 1835 said:

> "The cotton is principally bought and sold by sample,—the purchasers very rarely considering it necessary to examine the bulk. By strict probity and honour invariably observed by the brokers in their dealings with each other, this immense business is conducted with a facility and dispatch which have probably no parallel in any other market in the world, and which could not exist to the same extent in the sale of any other description of merchandise."[103]

[102] Hunt, *Merchants' Magazine*, 1843, VIII, p. 556.
[103] Baines, *Cotton Manufacture*, 1835, p. 319.

DIRECT PURCHASES BY THE MANUFACTURER OR SPINNER

The possibilities of securing for themselves the profits obtained by the various intermediaries who handled the cotton on its way from America to the mill, must have early attracted the attention of some of the spinners, particularly of those whose capital resources were sufficiently large to enable them to dispense with the long- or short-time credit afforded by the dealer and the importer.

There is an instance recorded of the interest of the firm of McConnel and Kennedy in this line. As early as 1806 a Charleston commission merchant had visited Manchester and had tried to convince the firm of the desirability of this method of purchase. After his return to the United States he kept in touch with them by means of periodic reports, not unlike the brokers' circulars issued in Liverpool. It seems to have been an effective advertising medium, for in 1807 a trial order was placed with the commission merchant in Charleston, although there is no proof that the order was fulfilled.

Shortly afterwards the embargo on American trade was imposed, and there are no further suggestions of direct purchases until 1809. In August of that year another order was given, which again had to be postponed owing to the passage of the Non-Intercourse Act. An order was finally placed in 1811, which does not seem to have resulted in any great gain to the concern.[104] A letter from a Savannah commission merchant to the Manchester firm, under date of April, 1815, shows the general way in which such transactions might be effected:

"Peace having taken place between this country and Great Britain we take the liberty of renewing our correspondence with you, and to offer our services as commission merchants in the purchase of cotton, and the disposal of goods which you may address to our care. Should you direct us to make purchases of cotton on your account, we would recommend you to nominate some substantial house at the northward to endorse our Bills on you and dispose of them here, and on whom we could pass drafts for purchases made, with greater facility than disposing of our Bills on you here. This practice has been pursued here and has been found to answer every purpose . . ."[105]

[104] Daniels, "Records," *Econ. Journal,* vol. XXV, p. 180.
[105] Daniels, *Cotton Trade under the Embargo,* Am. H. R., 1916, vol. XXI, p. 284.

But some of the spinners are said to have had their own houses in New Orleans and elsewhere for the purchase of the cotton.[106] Whether this means actual branch offices of the firm, or whether it refers to American houses acting as agents is impossible to determine. Mr. Wylie, whose evidence has already been cited, stated that "our principal business is the purchase of Cotton for account of English spinners." He also mentioned that he was connected with a house in New Orleans.[107] This would indicate a pretty complete organisation consisting of a commission merchant in Liverpool directing the operations of another commission merchant in New Orleans. Smithers stated more positively than any other writer the growing importance of the manufacturer. He wrote:

"The English manufacturers are gradually becoming the principal exporters and importers, the British merchant, comparatively, having no existence in this branch of trade but as a commission agent. This port, extensive as its commerce in the article of cotton may appear, is gradually becoming only the medium of shipping and receiving the returns, under the direct orders of the manufacturers of Manchester, Leeds, Birmingham, Sheffield, and other manufacturing districts."[108]

I find it difficult to accept the statement so baldly presented above. There seems to be too much evidence of the importance of the commission merchant and the regular importing merchant. And I further doubt if the manufacturing class were able, even granting that it had piled up huge surpluses, to assume the risks attendant upon the importation of cotton, particularly before the system of dealing in futures became customary, and gave to the buyer of spot cotton in America insurance against the risk of fluctuation in price before the cotton could be landed.

But it does appear evident that many of the manufacturers did import on their own account, possibly with a desire to secure exactly the grade of cotton they desired, or possibly with a view to speculation. Never, however, in this period did it become the characteristic method of securing cotton.

This desire to speculate might be satisfied in the home market, and speculation was indulged in by many of the spinners, as well

---

[106] Parl. Papers, Report on Orders in Council, 1812 (210), p. 355.

[107] Parl. Papers, Report on Commercial Distress, 1847-1848, XXIV (31), p. 227.

[108] Smithers, *Liverpool*, 1825, p. 139.

as the dealers, brokers, and others. Any cotton bought in the market by a broker for his own purposes and not for a client was for speculative purposes—to hold for a rise. And in the cotton market reports it was often noted that, say, 4,000 of the total number of bales bought were bought on speculation.[109] A witness in 1833 stated that the majority of the cotton spinners supplied themselves regularly and periodically with their current supplies, but that some of the wealthier spinners speculated. He mentioned having heard of certain spinners with stocks which would serve them for six months; others with supplies sufficient for twelve months. This he considered not the business of the manufacturer or spinner, but speculation.[110]

[109] For example, cf. *New Orleans Price Current*, November 5, 1825, quoting the Liverpool Market Report of September 10.

[110] Parl. Papers, Report on Manufactures, 1833, p. 651.

CHAPTER IV

THE ORGANISATION OF THE AMERICAN COTTON TRADE

IN the years before the development of the railroad, little cotton was shipped overland from the plantation to the market. The state of the roads during a great part of the year made the cost of such transportation prohibitive. If the plantation were located on a navigable stream, the crop was usually floated to the seaboard and sold there, or shipped by water to one of the many inland assembling points. In the case of plantations not having access to the waterways, some hauling by wagon was necessary, but this was reduced to a minimum. The cotton was hauled to one of these assembling points, which were usually located on a river, and thence shipped to a port on the Atlantic or the Gulf of Mexico. The condition of the waterways was, therefore, of great importance to the planter and to the factor. Too much water or too little water might keep cotton from the market during a favorable season, and occasion great loss.[1]

There were many inland shipping or assembling points in this period. One of them, about which we shall have more to say later, was Augusta, Georgia, located on the Savannah River, two hundred and forty miles above the city of Savannah. The baled cotton from the surrounding plantations was brought to Augusta in wagons or on small rivercraft, and shipped from Augusta to Savannah, there to be reshipped in ocean-going vessels, bound for a European or a northern American port.

---

[1] *Cf.* Trotter, *Observations*, 1839, p. 103.

"The circumstance, even, of an insufficient supply of water in the rivers to enable the drawers of bills of exchange to ship their cotton to the factors at the outports in time to meet their bills, has been stated as materially adding to the distresses of the winter of 1836, although the crop of that year was unusually large, and the prospects in the autumn most promising."

In general the cotton was pressed on the plantation, at the plantation gin press, and it remained in this state until it reached the terminal port. It was stated that in Georgia about half of the cotton was packed for market on the plantation in sacks resembling meal bags: such packages of cotton were called "round bales." The other half was packed in awkward bales, called "square bales." By the time the bales had reached the port, neither kind was in a condition to permit of further transportation, and it was therefore necessary to recompress the bales at the port.[2] For this purpose steam presses were erected, and the bales were compressed at a charge of about fifty cents per bale. Mobile is said to have had cotton presses with a capacity of 168,000 bales monthly, and other ports had facilities more or less proportionate to the demand for their services.[3] The total expense of this re-pressing at the port was considerable, but it was probably the most economical arrangement, in view of the cost of installing sufficiently powerful presses on the plantation.

THE COTTON FACTOR AND THE PLANTER

During the first half of the nineteenth century, and in general up to the Civil War, the Southern planter had three ways of marketing his cotton. He might consign it directly to a Northern or European market and have it sold for him by an agent; he might ship the cotton to the nearest port, and have it sold there by commission merchants or factors; or he might sell the cotton through a cotton factor at the inland assembling point.

It is the general purpose of this chapter to examine these three methods of distribution, to determine if possible the method which seems characteristic, the reasons for it, and the changes in method which developed during the period from 1800 to 1850. We shall begin first with a discussion of the operations of the factor, not attempting to distinguish too closely between the inland factor and the port factor, as their operations are in most cases identical.

The system of marketing by factors or commission houses in America was not peculiar to cotton (although possibly it attained a greater degree of development in the cotton trade than

[2]DeBow, *Review*, 1847, III, p. 19.
[3] Hunt, *Merchants' Magazine*, 1851, XXIV, p. 266.

in any other), but was common to all the staple products of the
South, as well as of other parts of the United States. Tobacco,
rice, grain, provisions, and many other products were exported
or sold for domestic consumption by commission merchants.

During the Colonial period, much of the factorage business
seems to have been in the hands of British merchants. When the
Revolution destroyed their business, their places were taken by
the more important merchants and business men of Richmond,
Charleston, and other cities (who in many cases had already established a small factorage business, either for themselves or as
correspondents), or by others attracted by the possible profits
and by the respectable social position which attached to the
business.[4]

General Relations. The relations between the cotton factor
and the planter were intimate, friendly, and enduring. The factor was something more than the business agent of the planter;
he was his close business and social friend. This relationship
naturally led the factor to act upon other considerations besides
the financial condition of the planter and the security he might
offer. Millions of dollars, it is said, were advanced by the Southern factors on the mere personal word of the planter, with no
formal security at all, and with only a memorandum to record
the amounts involved.[5]

This close association of the factor and the planter was an
invariable feature of the Southern organisation. In the first
place the distance of the planters from the markets, their consequent inability personally to oversee the sale of their cotton, and
their general lack of information as to the conditions in the
world markets, made it advisable to employ the services of a
specialist.[6]

The System of Advances. But, aside from this phase, which
would explain the existence of some sort of an agent, the pe-

---

[4] Stone, ''Cotton Factorage System,'' *Am. Hist. Rev.*, 1915, vol. XX, p.
558.

South in Rebuilding, vol. V, p. 403.

[5] Stone, ''Cotton Factorage System,'' *Am. Hist. Rev.*, 1915, vol. XX, p.
559.

[6] One of the functions of the factor was to keep his client informed, to
the best of his ability, of the state of the foreign markets. Bostwick (see p.
71) was in the habit of sending out circulars to a regular list of customers
as soon as he himself received news of the Liverpool quotations, but they
took a long time to reach him. On November 18, 1826, he sent out a

culiar dependence of the planter on the agent (rather than the dependence of the agent on the planter) arose from the practical necessity of securing funds to carry on the work of the plantation until the crop was harvested and sold. The lack of banking facilities, and the absence of security which would be readily available as a pledge, offered to the factor an opportunity to act as a banker to the planter, taking his growing or to-be-grown cotton as security. It is not, however, within our province to inquire into the causes of the dependence of the planter on the factor; it is sufficient to show that this was the case, and to indicate, if possible, in what ways it affected the general organisation.

One cannot read the contemporary writings of this period, or even scan the advertisements in the newspapers, without realising very vividly to what an extent the long-credit system permeated the entire business structure of the South. Trotter, in 1839, noted that the growers of rice and tobacco depended chiefly on the Southern Atlantic cities, while

"The cotton planters usually obtain advances for the purchases of their slaves and the improvement of their plantations from the merchants or factors of New Orleans, or other ports on the Gulf of Mexico. They are supplied with clothing for slaves, and other necessary articles of consumption, on credit, by the smaller country traders, who procure them on a still longer credit from the merchants of the Atlantic cities."[7]

But the necessity for giving long credits to the planters made it necessary, of course, for the merchants, retail and wholesale, to secure credits from the importing houses or the Northern manufacturers over an equally long or even longer period. To this system was ascribed the economic slavery of the South to the North, which received much notice in the middle of the century.

"Their [i.e., the planters'] habit of laying out their incomes before they get them and requiring a credit in all their dealings for the year, till the close of it, or until they sell their crops, even if it be longer, is the root of the whole evil of our system of credit. . . . If the planters

circular giving the Liverpool quotations of some time in September; on November 25 the quotations of the 17th of October; December 9 those of October 24. Quotations were generally at least six weeks old before they came into the hands of the planter.

7 Trotter, *Observations*, 1839, p. 33.

require a long credit, the merchants, wholesale and retail thru whom they are supplied, would at least require an equally long credit, so far as they purchase upon credit. A large money capital thus becomes necessary for the importing merchants, that a long credit may be extended to the planters, who, so far from really requiring credit, own the whole capital which pays for our entire annual importations!"[8]

Besides the high interest rates which the planter had to pay for his advances, he was required to pay credit prices for the goods which he bought of the port or local dealer. Tompkins notes that the planter bought provisions, for example, entirely on credit, and was forced to pay a price of twenty cents per pound for bacon, when the cash price was but twelve cents a pound; and he was charged for other things in proportion. As the average credit for such purchases was four months, the planter paid interest at the rate of about two hundred per cent per annum.[9]

Advances of funds might be made by the port factors and commission houses on the security of cotton consigned to them for sale. The following advertisements, taken from the *New Orleans Price Current* in 1848, show the general nature of the business at these terminal points:

"Jackson, Washington and Company, Cotton Factors and Commission Merchants, 75 Camp St. Advances made on Consignments to their house (Todd, Jackson, and Company) in Liverpool.
>   Bagging and Rope
>   Braintree Improved Gins
>   Kentucky Jeans and Linseys."

"Dunlop, Moncure and Company, in general commission business in Richmond, solicit consignments of Sugar, Molasses, Bacon, etc., will advance two-thirds of market value."

"Poole, James M. Commission and Forwarding Merchant and Cotton Factor, No. 90 Magazine Street.

*   *   *   *   *

"Cash advances made upon shipments of Cotton, Sugar, Bagging, etc., consigned to the Above, or for sale here, to the amount of three-fourths of fair market value."[10]

---

[8] DeBow, *Review*, 1847, IV, p. 221.

[9] Tompkins, D. A., "Money in Cotton Growing," in *Southern States*, July, 1897.

[10] *New Orleans Price Current*, January 19, 1848.

"Advances made on consignments of Cotton and other Produce to

Messrs Hicks and Company   New York
   "   Bates and Company   Boston
   "   De Laroche Arm'd Delessert and Company   Havre
   "   George Moore and Company   Trieste

And my correspondents in London and Liverpool.

Wm. Mure, 118 Common Street."[11]

These are fairly representative advertisements. It will be noted that, in all the cases cited, advances on consignments were offered as an inducement. This was not the case always. In the issue of the *New Orleans Price Current* of October 7, 1848, we find advertisements of 343 firms of cotton factors, commission merchants, general agents, etc. Of these, thirty-two advertised that they gave advances. This ratio is not, however, of any particular significance, because of the fact that in the number given, there were probably many firms that were too small to be able to do much in the way of making advances, and who therefore handled only a small proportion of the business, and many, doubtless, who gave advances did not think it necessary to mention it.

It will also be noticed that the amount of the advances ranged between two-thirds and three-fourths of the market value of the produce. Few firms stated definitely what they were willing to offer, but it is believed that this was about the average amount. We have already seen that it was the proportion common in the Liverpool cotton market.

It seems safe to assume that practically all of the commission houses were prepared to make advances, and that the majority of the planters were in the habit of receiving advances at some time or other in their career.

But not only did the port factors make advances; the planters might have recourse to one of the many factors located at an inland assembling point.

A valuable collection of business records of Mr. William Bostwick has been deposited in the Yale University Library. It consists of letter books, account books, and miscellaneous memorandum books. Of these, by far the most valuable are the letter books, giving a manuscript copy of the letters of Bostwick to his various customers in the country and in other places. Bost-

11 *New Orleans Price Current,* October 7, 1848.

wick was in business in Augusta, Georgia, from 1826 until 1848, under various partnership names, as E. C. Campbell and Company, Bostwick and Baird, etc., but it is obvious that he was the leading member of whatever firm he formed. During the early part of his business career in Georgia he was in the cotton "commission and warehouse" business: in other words, he was a factor at an inland assembling point. It is from these records that much of the material relative to the operations of inland factors is derived.

On June 1, 1826, the partnership of Campbell and Bostwick was formed, under the name of E. C. Campbell and Company, and notice was given the public that the new firm would engage in the warehouse and commission business, and would be able to make advances to customers when required. On June 13 the first advance was noted—of $115 to a Mr. Jenkins, against receipt of cotton. In a letter of October 3, 1826, Bostwick wrote to his partner:

"I have been generally among our customers in the country, and so far from being disposed to quit us, they are doing what they can to get others to store with us—of the large amount of our advances there is not one but what is good—I presume we shall realise a considerable part of our advances during the winter."[12]

Again, in a letter to a Mr. Dunbar, who was seeking an advance, he reiterated his willingness to make advances. He said:

"The advance you apply for of Cash $150 and 10 bushels of salt you have not informed us on what account it is to be made nor how it is to be met—on cotton stored with us we are always ready to make advances and to hold the cotton to secure the best market price."[13]

Advances were for different periods according to the customs of the particular locality. In Augusta they were for sixty or ninety days. Bostwick, writing under date of May 12, 1832, of a delinquent debtor, said:

"The fact is that the whole of this demand was for cash advanced three or four years since for his accommodation (understood to be as it always is in the Warehouse business for 60 to 90 days, or at the extent of the winter) and all we ever charged him was the customary commission of 2½ per cent."[14]

12 Bostwick, Letter Book, I, October 3, 1826.
13 *Ibid.*, I, October 8, 1828.
14 *Ibid.*, I, May 12, 1832.

In a public letter of the firm of Bevans and Humphreys of Philadelphia, we note that they offered to allow anyone who should ship cotton to the house of Humphreys and Biddle (in Liverpool) to draw bills on them at sixty days sight for two-thirds of the market price of the cotton. These bills would be accepted by Bevans and Humphreys, when accompanied by the bills of lading, and could be readily discounted in the market.[15]

An indication of a longer term of credit is given in the following quotation. Possibly it is true that in the Mississippi district longer credits were given, but there is reason to believe that the competition for consignments at this time was keen, and the long term was possibly offered as an additional inducement.

"The directors of the Mississippi Union Bank at Natchez, have issued a circular in which they say that believing the cotton crop of that state will be short, they will make advances to the planters who desire to postpone their sales till this can be ascertained, at the rate of sixty dollars per bale of four hundred pounds, upon the delivery of same to the bank's agents at the different shipping points on the Mississippi, with a note payable twelve months after date, endorsed by two or more good securities."[16]

Further evidence of the longer credits obtaining at about the same time is found in a circular letter issued in October, 1838, by John Ingersoll, who claimed to be the agent of Humphreys and Biddle in Liverpool; he offered to make advances to anyone consigning cotton to the Liverpool firm, and guaranteed to hold it until the following summer, when he believed the price would be more favorable.[17]

As has been seen, the advance might be in the form of cash or in bills of exchange, or it might be in goods. Bostwick advanced cash to a number, and in some cases he accepted and paid bills drawn against him.[18] The bank of the above quota-

[15] *Financial Register*, II, p. 380. Letter dated December 7, 1838.

[16] *Financial Register*, 1838, II, p. 380. This occurs in the period when speculation in cotton on the part of the banks was at its height, when Mr. Nicholas Biddle with his reorganised United States Bank and the Liverpool office were bidding for consignments.

[17] *Financial Register*, 1838, II, p. 379. A circular dated October 22, 1838, and issued from Natchez.

[18] *Cf.* letter of July 22, 1826. "Your draft of $300 we have accepted, and that for $143.91 we will pay as you direct from the sales of the cotton." (Letter Book, I.) Again on November 14, 1828: "Since the 30th Sept, we

tion evidently gave its advance in the form of cash, or possibly a deposit, and took two-name paper as security.

The system of advances, as described above, differed little from the systems in vogue in Liverpool and in other markets where commission business was general. In the South it reached a much greater development than elsewhere, and proceeded along still different lines. For, not only were funds advanced against shipments of cotton—a normal mercantile procedure almost everywhere—but loans were made to the planters on the basis of growing cotton, or cotton about to be planted.[19] An article in the *Financial Register* stated:

"Everybody knows that the cotton planters of the Southwestern states, procure large supplies of clothing for their slaves, of every article required for their own consumption, upon credit from the neighboring merchants, in anticipation of the next year's crop, . . ."[20]

Again, a writer in DeBow's *Review*, in 1849:

have received no cotton from you which has left us for some time in advance of your drafts. You will recollect you advised us they would be met at maturity either with cotton or funds remitted us." (Letter Book, I.)

[19] While there seems to be little doubt as to the existence of this practice of mortgaging the growing crop, and the crop as yet unplanted, the legality of a mortgage on the latter is open to suspicion.

No early court decisions on this subject have been found, and the later court decisions are quoted with the realisation that they do not in themselves settle the problem raised.

The following quotation refers to the legality of a mortgage on growing crops, and is taken from the summary of Stephens vs. Tucker, 55 Georgia 543, July, 1875.

"A mortgage may be of part of a growing crop, if the part mortgaged be so described as to be identified by parol evidence. . . ."

In the case of G. A. Redd and Company vs. Burrus and Williams (58 Georgia 574, January, 1877) it was held that a mortgage on unplanted cotton was invalid. "There can be no valid sale or mortgage of a portion of a crop not planted and therefore an obligation dated the 25th of December, 1874, to deliver certain cotton of the next year's crop—the crop of 1875—passed no title to the obligee."

The same conclusion seems to have been reached in a case decided in South Carolina in the same year. But it is stated that "although a mortgage on property to be subsequently acquired may not be valid or effectual at the time it is given, yet if the mortgagee take the property into his possession after it is acquired and before the rights of others as creditors or purchasers have attached thereon, the right to the mortgaged property passes from the mortgagor to the mortgagee." (Moore vs. Byrum, 10 South Carolina Rich. 452.)

[20] *Financial Register*, 1837, vol. I, p. 63.

"The greatest drawback upon the cotton planters' interest is the yearly practice of drawing bills upon the coming crop."[21]

In 1838 some of the banks in Mississippi were offering to advance sixty dollars a bale on cotton, "forty on the present and twenty on the coming crop.[22] A writer in Hunt's *Merchants' Magazine* noted that "frequently the planters of the South procure from the merchants of New York advances on their crops, even while growing upon the fields."[23]

It was this phase of the system of advances which made the relations of the planter and the factor so enduring and binding. In the first place, in order to give the factor a reasonable degree of security, the planter who had received a loan from a factor was required to plant so many acres in cotton, calculated to produce so many bales. He was further required to ship all of his production to the factor, even if a smaller quantity would have liquidated his indebtedness, and finally there was the so-called "penalty system," by which the planter agreed to pay, in addition to the customary commission for sales and interest on the loan, a forfeit of a certain account per bale, previously agreed upon—running as high as four dollars per bale—for each bale by which his actual production fell short of the number of bales he had contracted to ship.[24]

The interest rate on such loans to the planters probably ran rather high, although it varied according to the place and the state of the loan market. Stone stated that it ranged between eight and twelve per cent. He added:

"It was usually charged only as funds were actually drawn, though in some instances it was computed on the face of the loan, regardless of the average time of its actual use by the borrower. There was also

21 DeBow, *Review*, 1849, VII, p. 412.

22 *Financial Register*, 1838, vol. II, p. 268.

23 Hunt, *Merchants' Magazine*, 1841, IV, p. 224.

24 Stone, "Cotton Factorage System," *Am. Hist. Rev.*, 1915, XX, pp. 561-563.

Hammond, *The Cotton Industry*, 1897, pp. 288-289.

In a fairly recent case decided in the Georgia Supreme Court it was held that a "contract by which one of the parties agrees to ship to the other, who is a cotton factor and commission merchant, a certain number of bales of cotton within a stipulated period, or in default thereof to pay to the other $1.00 per bale for every bale short of that number is not *per se* usurious." (Georgia Law Reports, 90 Ga. 590. MacKensie vs. Flannery and Company, 1892.) This case shows the persistence of the "penalty system."

in some cases a customary fee of from one-half of one per cent to two and one-half per cent added to the interest charge."[25]

The Factor as the Selling Agent for the Planter. The cotton began to come to market in October, and shipments continued from then until the beginning of the summer. As cotton was sent from the plantation to Bostwick in Augusta it was often sold immediately, in many cases for cash, and the funds were placed at once at the disposal of the shipper. If the market was not in a favorable state, Bostwick had warehouses in which he could store the cotton and wait for better times. Or, if he believed that the market in Augusta might be inferior to the Savannah market, he would ship to an agent in Savannah, with instructions to sell at the best price obtainable.

The quickest and probably the least expensive method was to sell the cotton on the wagon. To one customer Bostwick wrote that the best he could get offered "on the wagon was eight and one-half cents," but that later he sold it in the warehouse for eight and five-eighths cents. A market report of the cotton trade in Augusta, quoted in a New Orleans paper, noted that the business "is still confined to the streets, and very little coming in is stored."[26] In Charleston, when trade began to revive after the war of 1812, extensive wagon yards were laid off for the convenience of the planters and farmers. The cotton was either purchased out of the wagons, or bartered for goods. A large

---

[25] Stone, "Cotton Factorage System," *Am. Hist. Rev.*, 1915, XX, 560.

It will be remembered that Bostwick mentioned that he charged his delinquent debtor only the customary fee of two and one-half per cent, and had made no charge for interest as such.

It is somewhat of a question as to whether it was ever a custom to charge both interest and a commission on the advance. In the case of Cheeseborough vs. Hunter (S. C. Law Reports, 1 Hill 400) in 1833 the plaintiff attempted to prove that it was the custom, and to collect a commission of two and one-half per cent in addition to the interest charges. It is stated that two witnesses were produced. "The first had known instances in which they were charged, and others in which they were not, and considered the charge correct. The other had dealt largely with factors, and never paid commissions on advances, and they were not usually charged, so that no usage was proved." In this case it was held that it had not been proved to be the custom to charge both interest and a commission, but it is evident that cases where both were charged were not unknown. A very exhaustive study of other court decisions would be necessary before one could state authoritatively whether or not this double charge obtained generally in the cotton states of the South.

[26] *New Orleans Price Current*, October 24, 1835.

trade of this sort developed without the intermediation of the factor; nevertheless, the planter soon found it to his advantage to employ the factor.[27]

But the cotton was often warehoused and kept for a favorable market. Bostwick wrote to one client that he was always willing to put cotton in his warehouse and hold it until he could secure a good price.[28] To another he wrote that in spite of having exposed his samples in the market for a week he had not been able to get the price he wanted.[29] The amounts that might be held even in the warehouses of an inland centre were quite considerable. Bostwick himself had in his warehouses on one occasion over 2,000 bales.[30] Writing to a New York firm he noted in 1834 that "there is rising 100,000 bales not to be sold in this market," the reason being that the planters were not allowing it to be sold for the prevailing price.[31] Later in the same year he estimated the quantity held in the warehouses at about 50,000 bales.[32]

Little light is thrown by these letters on the question as to whether Bostwick dealt in cotton on his own account or not. Shortly after the partnership of Bostwick and Campbell was formed, the warehouse was struck by lightning and burned. Bostwick sent out a circular letter advising his clients of "the melancholy circumstance," and extended them his sympathy and "hope that you may have divine support in so severe an affliction."[33] There is no indication that he lost, other than by the burning of the building; all seems to have fallen on the holders of cotton, who were evidently not insured, for later in the same month we find a general circular sent to his customers giving the details of a plan of insurance "upon all cotton in store by which you perceive we can have your cotton insured from the time of receiving it in the warehouse at the rate of one cent a bale per week."[34] While it would therefore appear as if Bostwick acted only as a commission agent in the sale of cotton, I do not believe we can consider this negative evidence as at all

27 Fraser, Charles, *Reminiscences*, 1854, pp. 12-16.
28 Letter Book, I, October 8, 1828.
29 *Ibid.*, II, May 30, 1835.
30 *Ibid.*, I, Circular dated August 10, 1826.
31 *Ibid.*, II, January 29, 1834.
32 *Ibid.*, II, February 10, 1834.
33 *Ibid.*, I, August 10, 1826.
34 *Ibid.*, I, August 30, 1826.

conclusive, although the commission business was doubtless his main concern. Certainly Bostwick was too shrewd a business man to neglect any opportunity to make a profit in buying cotton out-right simply because he was, theoretically, a factor only.

In a court decision of 1822, involving a factor, it was stated that:

"Factors of every description often sell for themselves. With our factors, selling rice and cotton, it is often that they are the planters, and may be speculators in the produce too."[35]

Commission on Sales. The commission for selling cotton for the planter was, in most instances, a percentage based on the value of the cotton. So far as can be determined from the printed tariffs of Chambers of Commerce the maximum was pretty generally two and one-half per cent. This is the commission allowed by the Chambers of Commerce of New Orleans and of Charleston.[36] The tariff of charges agreed to in New Orleans in 1834 allowed as the commission on sales of sugar, molasses, cotton, tobacco, and lead, two and one-half per cent; on all other produce the rate was five per cent. That the rate was not necessarily uniform is shown by the following:

"We stated some weeks ago that the Commission on Merchants and Cotton Sellers in Savannah, had entered into an agreement to charge for the sale of cotton, after the 1st of August next, two and one-half per cent commission. It appears that some of the Commission Merchants refused to go into this arrangement. By reference to the card of the Savannah House, R. A. Allen and Son, it will be seen that they will continue to sell cotton at the old rates, that is, 50 cents a bag."[37]

Stone stated that although the usual commission for selling cotton was two and one-half per cent, in some places it rose as high as four per cent.[38]

[35] South Carolina Law Reports. Davenport vs. Riley, 2 McCord 200.

[36] DeBow, *Review*, 1847, III, p. 84. Tariff of Charges, etc., of New Orleans, Chamber of Commerce, agreed to November, 1846.

New Orleans Price Current, July 23, 1836, ditto April, 1834. (This tariff seems to have been in effect until 1846; in both the rate is two and one-half per cent.)

DeBow, *Review*, 1846, I, 450. Ditto for Charleston.

Niles, *Register*, vol. XXIII, p. 217.

[37] *Federal Union*, Milledgeville, Ga., June 16, 1857.

[38] Stone, "Cotton Factorage System," *Am. Hist. Rev.*, 1915, XX, p. 561.

The all-prevailing influence of credit in the Southern economy cannot but have had an unfavorable effect upon the Southern planter in many instances. To a certain extent his dependence on the factor robbed him of his

The Factor as a Purchasing Agent for the Planter. Besides making advances to the cotton planter, and selling his cotton for him, the factor also acted as his commission agent in the purchase of plantation supplies or other articles which he might want. In this respect he seems to a large extent to have taken the place of the local retail merchant. Bostwick noted in some of his letters that he was forwarding the goods ordered by a particular client, although the instances were not numerous until later, when he became a general storekeeper.

The advertisements in the newspapers show a general readiness on the part of the commission merchants to serve their clients in this capacity. The following illustrates the twofold nature of the business:

"Sloan and Byrne, Commission Merchants, New Orleans, will give their undivided attention to consignments to their address and will

most valuable right—the right to hold his cotton for a favorable market. Of course not all the planters were in this position; many of them could control the sale of their cotton, and could indicate to the factor the minimum price for which they were willing to sell. Some of Bostwick's customers evidently gave him directions as to the price at which he might sell. But it is probably true that the majority of the planters could not control the sales. One writer thus declaimed against the credit system:

"Draw bills! This bill business is the very thing that ruins us. *Keep out of debt and control your cotton.* . . . I know where seven cents was refused for a crop, and I had to take five cents." (DeBow, *Review*, 1849, VII, 411.)

He considered that the "greatest drawback upon the cotton planters' interest, is the yearly practice of drawing bills upon the coming crop," for:

"The planter is thereby forced to send his cotton forward, and the merchant wants the money to replace in the bank so as to get another loan for someone else, and he sells. Often he is compelled to sell and very often loses for his patron one or two cents." (DeBow, *Review*, 1849, VII, 412.)

Even when the commission merchant who had made advances did not sell the cotton in the home or port market, but reconsigned it to Liverpool or some other foreign market, or where a planter had himself consigned it directly to a foreign commission agent, there was a great possibility of loss. In most of these cases the foreign commission house would make advances to the American exporter. In order to protect himself, or to provide himself with funds for further ventures, the foreign agent might sell the cotton out at an unfavorable moment, judged from the standpoint of the American exporter, or he might make fictitious sales, in order to profit at the expense of the American shipper. On this point one writer stated:

"The financial system of advances is one no doubt by which the shippers of produce are generally victimised. The complaints were formerly long and loud against the 'slaughtering' of American tobacco and cotton in the foreign cities to which that was consigned on advance. The merchandise was

promptly execute all orders accompanied by cash or satisfactory credits."[39]

THE COTTON BUYERS

It is necessary to consider next the demand side of the cotton market. We have seen that most of the cotton came to the market in charge of factors who were acting for the real owner of the cotton. With whom did they come in contact, and to whom did they sell the cotton?

It is possible to distinguish several different classes of buyers, of varying degrees of importance. We have of course the local factor, who might appear on the demand side of the market, either as a private speculator, or in the more important capacity of agent for a Northern cotton shipper. We also have the representatives or branches of Northern or European cotton houses and the agents of the Lancashire spinning firms; and finally the Southern banks appeared as important purchasers and shippers of cotton in at least one period.

The same factor who sold cotton for the planter might appear as the buying agent for himself or a Northern firm. It was on this ground that a planter in 1849 objected to the scheme to make the commission merchants the agents of the planters with power to fix rates. It may be true that there was a separate class of buying factors; our evidence is too meagre to allow us to generalise on this point. Such evidence as we have, however, points to the practice of the factor both buying and selling in the same market, although he probably did not act as the buying and the selling agent in the same transaction.

Purchases by Local Commission Merchants for the Account of Others. The prevalence in Charleston around 1815 of the practice of purchasing on British account has already been pointed out.[40] Bostwick at one period in his career did extensive buying on a commission basis for Thaddeus Phelps and Company of New York. He bought the cotton in the local market, shipped it by river to his agent at Savannah, who then transshipped it to a vessel for New York. Thaddeus Phelps and Company sent

generally sold at the most unfavorable moment and circumstance and not infrequently bought in at the low figure thus produced, by the acceptor, to hold for his advantage." (*The Southern Trade*, May 2, 1860, p. 26.)

[39] *New Orleans Price Current*, December 9, 1837.

[40] Chapter III, p. 40.

him definite orders as to the number of bales they wanted, and the maximum price per pound they were willing to pay. Bostwick purchased the cotton, drew on the New York house at sixty days sight, and received as a commission for so doing, two and one-half per cent on the value.[41]

There is good reason to believe that this commission of two and one-half per cent was quite general. On one occasion Thaddeus Phelps and Company objected to paying a commission so high. Bostwick immediately replied as follows:

"I notice your remarks in relation to commission and in reply have to state that anything less that 2½% is not a compensation for the time and labor necessary. . . . It is I believe the customary commission here. I know of several who purchase largely that charge it, and I know of no responsible house that does it for less."[42]

The various tariffs of different Southern cities, already alluded to, took cognisance of the custom and specified exactly the rate which was applicable to the purchase and shipment of produce on foreign and domestic account. In the tariff of commissions for Charleston this item had first place, which would argue that at least that type of business was not of minor importance. The rate applicable to purchases and shipments for both foreign and domestic account was two and one-half per cent.

Besides the actual commission for purchasing there were additional charges collected by the commission merchant. The shipping charges on cotton were given as follows for Charleston:

Brokerage	12½ cents per bale
Marking	2 " " "
Mending	4 " " "
Mending, furnishing bagging and twine	10 " " "
Drayage	6¼ " " "
Wharfage	4 " " "

Storage while awaiting shipment, 8 cents per week per bale for the first and last weeks, and 4 cents for all intermediate weeks.[43]

Cotton purchased by a local commission agent, whether at the interior town, or at the port, was generally paid for by bills of

[41] Letter Book, II. Letters to Thaddeus Phelps and Company, particularly September, 1835.

[42] Letter Book, II, October 22, 1835.

[43] DeBow, *Review*, 1846, I, 450. Tariff of Commissions in Charleston.

exchange.[44] The commission merchant drew a bill on the Northern house, or the foreign house, as the case might be, and discounted the bill at the bank. The usual tenor of the bill was ten days, thirty days, or sixty days sight. Payment by bill of exchange meant an additional item to be added to the cost of shipping the cotton, for a charge of from one and one-half to two and one-half per cent for drawing bills on foreign houses, and from one to one and one-half per cent for drawing bills on domestic houses, was both allowed and customary.[45]

As a matter of practice probably few bills were drawn directly on the foreign houses. In the Southern cities there was little demand for sterling exchange—in which such bills would have been drawn—because of the fact that most of the imported goods came to the South through Northern ports and merchants. This, of course, caused a great demand for exchange on New York. A Liverpool merchant, when he wished a Charleston or New Orleans factor to purchase cotton for him, opened a credit with a New York mercantile or banking house, which thereafter authorised the Southern purchasing agent to draw bills of exchange on the New York firm. This enabled the Southern factor at times to sell his bills in the market at a premium, rather than at a discount.[46]

The occasional difficulty of securing bills on New York with which to pay for goods bought from New York is well illustrated in the case of Bostwick, who, when a general merchant, made very extensive purchases in New York and elsewhere. He wrote to a New York house, which seems to have been pressing him for payment, that in Augusta it was absolutely impossible to secure a single bill on New York, because of the fact that the cotton planters were holding their cotton for a rise, and that until they should begin to sell he could not make payment. Just why the banks were unable to draw bills is not clear, but it appears to have been a fact, for he remarked that "not a Bank nor a Broker will draw at sight, or at short sight, or on any terms. This is owing to the planters all holding on and no cotton is offered for sale—there is nobody drawing any bills."[47]

---

[44] "The New York merchant, when he orders his Charleston correspondents to purchase for him a cargo of cotton, directs him to draw on him for the amount, and these drafts he meets by bills on Liverpool drawn upon his agent there, who pays them out of the proceeds of the cotton when sold." (DeBow, *Review*, 1847, IV, p. 351.)

[45] DeBow, *Review,* 1846, I, p. 450. Tariff of Commissions for Charleston. Entz, *Exchange and Cotton Trade,* 1840, p. 16.

The following statement of the costs necessary to ship cotton from New York to Liverpool is taken from *Exchange and Cotton Trade,* 1840, p. 6, a manual intended for the use of the cotton exporter, and illustrates the various charges mentioned. The cotton is supposed to be shipped by the order of and for the account of a Liverpool merchant.

Cotton from New York to Liverpool.

100 Bales, weighing lbs. 38,500 at 11¢			$4,235.00
(No tare allowed)			
Brokerage 12½¢		$ 12.50	
Mending, etc.		14.25	
Cartage on board		12.50	39.25
			4,274.25
Marine Insurance on $4,702, including 10% imaginary profit, in series of 10 bales each in running numbers, at 1%		$ 47.02	
Policy		1.25	48.27
			4,322.52
Commission for purchasing, 2½%		$108.06	
Commission for drawing bills, 1½%		67.45	175.53
			$4,498.05

	£	s.	d.
Drawn on London at 60 days' sight, at the rate of $40 per £9, and 8% premium, in	£937	1	10
Banking Commission in London ½%		4 13	8

	£	s.	d.	£	s.	d.
Freight to Liverpool, at ½d per lb. on lb. 37,350 .	£77	16	3			
Primage, 5%	3	17	10			
Duty on cwt. 333.1.25 at 35d. per cwt. . . .	52	7	1			
Dock dues, £4.13.4; town dues £0.16.8	5	10	0			
Interest ½%	13	11		140	5	1

		£	s.	d.
Cartage, porterage, and weighing		3	18	0
Canvas, twine, and mending		1	15	0
Warehouse rent, 1d per week for 4 weeks . . .		1	13	4
Postages and small charges			8	7
Brokerage, ¼%	1⅞%			
Insurance against fire, ⅛%	£1,110.12	20	16	6
Discount of 3 months, 10 days, 1½%	on			

Commission and guarantee 3% not included

Total cost £1,110 12 0

Similar pro forma tables are given for Charleston, Savannah, Augusta, Mobile, and New Orleans, which differ but slightly from the above table.

[46] Entz, *Exchange and Cotton Trade,* 1840, p. 16. It was stated that New York exchange was usually at a premium in the Southern ports.

DeBow, *Review,* 1847, IV, p. 497. "In general exchanges on Europe are lowered by one or two per cent at the South . . ."

[47] Letter Book, II, January 17, 1834; January 29, 1834.

Purchases by Agents of Northern Mercantile and Manufac-turing Concerns. Besides securing cotton through the local commission merchants the business house located in the Northern cities might send its own agent to the South to make the purchases in person. These agents were provided with letters of credit, and authority to draw drafts on their employers to a certain amount; such drafts were drawn payable from sixty days to four months after sight. Few of them were dishonored, and they were purchased with great eagerness by those Southern merchants who wished to make remittances to the North. If the Northern merchant was purchasing for sale in the domestic market, he would receive the cotton in time to sell it and be in a position to meet the drafts at maturiy. If, on the other hand, he was purchasing to send abroad on consignment, or on order, then, as soon as he had received notice of the actual shipment of the cotton to Europe, he drew a draft on the merchant or commission merchant abroad for the whole or a large part of the value of the cargo. This draft could be readily sold to the importers of British goods, thus placing the merchant in a position to invest again.[48]

Another variation of the same method was described as being quite prevalent in the period around 1820. The merchant bargained with a bank for a loan to run for six months, offering such security as was required, and agreeing to pay the interest in advance and to receive the loan in the form of post notes of the bank, payable in ninety days. A further stipulation was that the post notes were to be put into circulation in the South.

For example, if a loan of $25,000 was made, the merchant sent his agent to Savannah, with letters of credit and proper authority for drawing bills of exchange on his principal. Upon arrival at Savannah, the agent immediately purchased a cargo costing $25,000, for which he paid $12,000 in the post notes of the bank, and for the remainder drew on the merchant in New York. The moment shipment was made he sent the bill of lading of the cargo to the principal. This enabled the merchant to draw on his commission merchant in Liverpool for about half the cost of the cargo, and dispose of the bill of exchange to an importer for cash, which was forthwith sent to the agent in the South. The process could be repeated almost indefinitely, and it was

[48] *Trade and Commerce of New York,* 1820, p. 32.

estimated that a merchant in New York could purchase and ship, in six weeks' time, cotton worth $100,000, with an initial capital of $25,000, and still be constantly in funds to meet his engagements.[49]

Undoubtedly a part of the cotton purchased by special agents sent to the South was on the account of the manufacturers of the North. A reference to this practice occurred in a New Orleans newspaper in 1838, but it does not give conclusive evidence:

"Buyers for the manufacturers of the North have been the most extensive operators this week, but there has been a considerable taken for English account also."[50]

The buyers referred to in the above quotation may have been the local commission merchants, or they may have been agents specially sent to the South to make purchases. We cannot state with any definiteness the prevalence of direct purchasing by Northern spinning mills, but it is believed that in this period the practice was not of very great importance, both because of the fact that there seem to be no references to it in contemporary literature, and because it is to be doubted if many of the spinning firms were in a position, financially, to purchase the cotton for ready money, as was the custom.[51]

Purchases by Agents of Foreign Houses. The third method of disposing of cotton was through purchases by agents of British or other foreign houses resident in the Southern or Northern cities. This practice has been discussed to some extent in the chapter on the organisation of the Liverpool market. It unquestionably existed. As early as 1812 we have evidence of the existence of correspondents and branch houses of the British firms in various markets in the United States. One individual stated that he had correspondents in Charleston, in New York,

[49] *Trade and Commerce of New York*, 1820, pp. 33, 35.
[50] *New Orleans Price Current*, January 27, 1838.
[51] *Cf*. Clarke, *Manufactures*, 1916, p. 366.
"On account of the competition of foreign buyers, cotton, wool, and similar commodities always moved quickly for cash or early payments, while the goods made from them sold on longer time. In 1849 southern staples commanded immediate returns, while northern manufactures sold on six or ten months' credit. Therefore it was difficult for early factory owners to procure materials without ready money, although it was impossible to dispose of goods for cash."

and one in Savannah; "at Charlestown and New York our chief correspondents reside."[52] In an article in DeBow's *Review*, mention was made of England's agents in this country "watching with keen eyes the annual growth of the cotton crop, and through their correspondents in the different localities, ascertaining the probable amount of production and home consumption."[53]

A typical advertisement in the Southern papers showing the connection of a local agent with foreign houses was as follows:

"ADVANCES The undersigned will make liberal advances on consignments of produce to their friends in London, Liverpool, New York, and Boston.
                    P. Maxwell and Company, 56 Magazine St."[54]

Most of the advertisements, however, did not mention any connection with foreign houses, and relatively few of them mentioned any connection with any other firms. It is true that there were a few cases in which firms offered to make advances on consignments to foreign houses, where the names of the foreign and the local house were so similar as to lead to the suspicion that one was a branch house of the other. For example, Hoghton, Rankin and Company of New Orleans, offered to advance on consignments of cotton and other produce, to Messrs. Rankin, Gilmour and Company of Liverpool. But these cases are very few indeed, and not at all typical.[55]

There is too some evidence leading one to believe that the establishment of foreign houses in the Southern cities was not customary; that, in so far as the foreign branches or agents were located in the United States, they were domiciled in the Northern cities, and carried on their trade with the South as an ordinary American firm in New York would. A writer on the possibility of establishing direct trade between the South and Europe lamented this lack of interest on the part of foreign purchasers

---

52 Parl. Papers, Report on Orders in Council, 1812 (210), p. 513. In general see Chapter III, pp. 42, 43.

53 DeBow, *Review*, 1852, XIII, p. 70.

54 *New Orleans Price Current*, October 7, 1848.

55 *New Orleans Price Current*, October 7, 1848. It is interesting to note that of the firms that mentioned outside connections, only seven spoke of their correspondents or houses in Liverpool, while fifteen solicited consignments for houses in New York, and fourteen for houses in Boston and elsewhere.

and sellers in the possible advantages of settling in the South.
He wrote:

"The foreign manufacturers, and the American planters, are equally
interested in establishing this system of direct exchange; and it can
only be effected by bringing the foreign manufacturers directly to the
cities of the cotton-growing states, and making these, instead of New
York, the great marts for vending foreign manufactures on the one
hand, and the raw material on the other. Considering the obvious
economy of this direct system of exchanges, *it seems strange that the
foreign manufacturers have not established their agencies, both for
selling goods, and purchasing cotton, in those cities in preference to
others.*"[56]

And, again:

"We know that before this trade was driven from our ports [South-
ern] . . . foreign capital to a very large amount was actually employed
in that trade—that British houses were established here, and that a very
successful business was thus, for a long time, carried on."[57]

But it is seemingly an impossible task to determine the relative importance of the foreign purchasing agents or branch
houses (mainly British, of course) in America. We have already
seen that the tendency in this period is for an increasingly great
proportion of all the cotton shipped to Liverpool to be shipped
on British account, but no sources are available which will assist us to generalise with any degree of exactness as to the total
amount purchased by the British representatives in the Southern
market, the amount purchased by Southern commission houses,
acting as the agents of foreign houses, the amount purchased by
them for the New York or other Northern houses, and the amount
purchased by agents of the Northern shipping firms.

Each of these methods was important, but we cannot prove
which was predominant. Nevertheless, contemporary Southern
sources give a strong impression of the overwhelming importance
of New York in both the export and import trade of the South.
This dependence of the South on the North was a complaint
very frequently heard, particularly near the middle of the century, and various plans were put forth as solutions of the problem. In a report made to the legislature of Alabama it was
stated that the entire amount of the exports of cotton from Ala-

[56] DeBow, *Review*, 1847, IV, p. 217. (Italics inserted.)
[57] *Ibid.*, p. 352.

bama which reached the European market had to pass through the hands of agents who were not citizens of the state.[58] The writer asserted:

"This immense amount [of commissions, etc.] . . . is distributed among those who act as the transporting and selling agents of the producer, all of whom live north of the Potomac river. The South thus stands in the attitude of feeding from her own bosom a vast population of merchants, shipowners, capitalists, and others, who without the claims of her progeny, drink up the life-blood of her trade."[59]

With reference to the trade with the Northern manufacturing states, the complaint was made that the trade passed through New York to the prejudice of the interests of both parties.

"This view of the subject causes us to regret that the extensive trade we carry on with the manufacturing States of the North, exchanging our raw cotton for their various manufactures—a trade highly important to both parties—is not carried on directly between the cities of the planting and manufacturing States, but *like our foreign commerce,* indirectly through the city of New York. Almost the whole of our immense exchanges center there; . . ."[60]

Again in a case involving shipments of cotton abroad it was stated that:

"Some of the complaints that are made in behalf of defendants have arisen from that unhappy course of trade which has allowed New York to become an intermediate toll-house for the imports and exports of Charleston to and from foreign ports."[61]

Other references might be given, but are withheld because it is hardly possible to prove by reference alone that most of the staples, whether for domestic or for foreign consumption, were directed to the final market from New York. It is nevertheless believed that most of the cotton exported from the Southern states was purchased for export either by Southern commission agents, acting for the New York shippers—American or British —or by agents sent from the North to purchase the cotton, and

[58] DeBow, *Review,* 1847, IV, pp. 339-340, note.
[59] *Ibid.,* p. 340, note.
[60] *Ibid.,* 1847, IV, p. 225. (Italics inserted.)
[61] South Carolina Law Reports, 1851, Kohtman vs. Brown and Goldsmith, 4 Rich. 479.

that the weight of British buying was felt through the North, rather than directly.[62]

THE COTTON BROKERS

We have seen that in the Liverpool market the common method of bringing buyer and seller together was through buying and selling brokers. There is reason to believe that brokers existed in the larger Southern markets. Two writers and students of the cotton trade and industry have asserted that the Southern factor sold his cotton through the broker. Hammond stated:

"The Southern factor disposed of his cotton through a broker, paying him a commission therefor of usually $1.50 a bale, but the broker paid out of this the commission to the Northern broker. The cotton thus sold was usually bought by similar factors or importing merchants at Northern ports."[63]

Stone likewise claimed that the brokers were the middlemen between the factor and the purchaser. He asserted:

"In the early days cotton sales were effected through a broker who acted as a middleman between the factor and the resident agent of a foreign mill, or merchant. To this broker was paid a commission of one half of one per cent, nominally borne by the mill agent. In practice and custom, however, one half of this commission was paid by the factor and charged to the planter. This was supposed to be divided between the factor and the broker."[64]

In the face of this authority I do not feel in a position to assert with any degree of positiveness my own belief on this question. But I would state that I am confident that both Hammond and Stone have somewhat overstated the case.

[62] On this point, as on another to be noted later—the brokerage question—it seems very difficult to know exactly where to turn for evidence. The periodical literature, especially of the South, where the question of the economic servitude of the South to the North was of great interest, would lead us to believe that practically all of the trade took place through the medium of New York.

Advertisements, directories, and such possible contemporary sources either are not available or reveal little. Statistics of exports of cotton from Southern and Northern ports to Great Britain are believed to be of no significance at all, for it is obvious that much of the cotton purchased by Northern houses could more economically be shipped from the Southern ports.

[63] Hammond, *The Cotton Industry,* 1897, p. 289.

[64] Stone, "Cotton Factorage," *Am. Hist. Rev.,* XX, 1915, p. 561.

It cannot be doubted that brokers existed in the cotton markets—at least in the large terminal markets. A report of a court decision in 1840 spoke of cotton brokers, but there is little to indicate that their business was different from that of a factor. The following is the summary of the facts in the case as given in the report:

"Defendant having about $4,000 desired to invest it in Cotton for Speculation. He accordingly applied to plaintiffs who were cotton brokers in the city of Charleston, and they purchased for him 316 bales; procured an advance on their own responsibility of $12,470 to pay for the cotton so produced; shipped it on board the Josepha (a vessel designated by defendant), and consigned it, according to the usages of trade to a house in Liverpool. Subsequent to the sailing of the vessel, the defendant refused to complete the contract. Upon this refusal this action was commenced. Verdict for plaintiffs, $4,000. *Held* that the defendant was liable to the plaintiff as vendor; that there was a sale and a delivery; and a new trial was refused."[65]

We find a number of brokers who advertised in the *New Orleans Price Current*. In the issue of January 19, 1848, the following different classes of brokers advertised:

Kind	*Number*
General Produce Brokers	3
Merchandise Brokers	3
Tobacco Brokers	2
Purchasing broker in Lead, Hemp, bagging and Rope, Grain, Flour, Provisions and Western Products generally; Selling Broker in Coffee, Salt, Foreign and Northern Merchandise	1
Produce Purchasing Broker	1
Sugar and Molasses Broker	1
Commission Merchant and General Produce Broker	1
Merchandise and Produce Broker	1
Purchasing Broker	1
General Broker	1
Total	15

There were about three hundred commission merchants of all kinds advertising in the same issue. Of course there is no conclusive deduction which legitimately may be drawn from the

[65] South Carolina Law Reports, 1840, Robertson vs. Shannon, 1 McMullan 164.

ratio, for we do not know how many commission houses or how many brokerage houses did not advertise. But it is, I think, significant, that there was no firm advertising its willingness to act as a broker, that specialised in the cotton brokerage business, or that even so much as mentioned cotton as one of the articles handled. Again, in some of the published tariffs of the Chambers of Commerce there was recognition of the fact that brokerage charges might be incurred. The New Orleans Chamber of Commerce tariff gave the list of commissions which might be charged and then stated: "the foregoing rates to be exclusive of Brokerage and Charges actually incurred."[66] The tariff of Charleston, however, did not mention brokerage charges except in connection with shipping, where it allowed for twelve and one-half cents a bale.[67] It seems not unlikely that this fee was for service rendered in securing space on a ship.

What seems most inexplicable is that in all the writings either of the period in question or of contemporary authors, with the exception of the writers already quoted, not a single reference to the brokerage system in cotton has been found. It cannot be claimed that an exhaustive survey of all possible sources has been made, but it is true that all of the readily available material has been combed with that point in view.

It is the writer's belief, based, it is true, on evidence of a negative character, that the broker in cotton was a person of minor importance in the trade in the first half of the nineteenth century; that, in general, factor dealt with factor or spinners' agents directly, without the intervention of the broker.

CONSIGNMENTS BY THE PLANTERS

Not all of the planters sold their cotton through a factor. Some of the larger planters were in a position to wait until the cotton could reach the foreign market to be sold. Others might consign their cotton to a Liverpool house directly and receive advances on their unsold cotton in much the same way that a regular shipping merchant would. But it is not believed that this method was ever very general, or very significant.

66 DeBow, *Review,* 1847, III, p. 84. Tariff of Charges, etc., agreed upon . . . by the New Orleans Chamber of Commerce, . . . November 2, 1846.

67 *Ibid.,* 1846, I, p. 450. Tariff of Charges, etc., agreed upon . . . by the Charleston Chamber of Commerce.

Gabriel Shaw, a witness before the Parliamentary Committee investigating, in 1833, the state of the manufactures, said of this practice:

"Our consignments are from planters and merchants, principally from merchants. The growers of cotton frequently consign themselves, but I believe that about three-fourths of the consignments are for account of mercantile houses."[68]

Baines, who published his work on the cotton trade only two years later, quoted this statement of Shaw with evident approval.[69]

Contemporary notices of shipments by the planters on their own account are infrequent, and when they do occur the language indicates the unusualness of the proceeding. The *Charleston Market Review* of May 1, 1826, noted that:

" '. . . Some of our Sea Island planters are disposed to ship their cotton on their own accounts and one crop, which heretofore has brought the highest rates in our markets, has been shipped by the planter in the course of the week.' "[70]

And again, on June 5:

"Some Sea Island Planters have preferred shipping their crops to selling them at these rates [25 to 30¢] and others are disposed to send them back to the country, to avoid expenses, until next season."[71]

It seems obvious that in these instances the reason for consignment was the low state of the Charleston market, and a belief that better terms might be obtained in Liverpool. A more striking statement is given in the following quotation from an article appearing in 1838:

"Letters from New Orleans state that the planters who last year were lured by the offer of large advances to become the shippers of their own cotton, have a terrible reverse in their affairs now. Cotton which might have been sold at $45 or $50 a bale, but which was shipped under advances of $60 a bale, has been sold and the returns made, showing a deficiency of $30 a bale, which the planters are now called upon to refund, and in much better money than they received. The letters say that few planters will be found stupid enough to be taken in that trap this year."[72]

[68] Parl. Papers, Report on Manufactures, 1833, VI (690), p. 93.
[69] Baines, *History of Cotton Manufacture*, 1835, p. 317.
[70] *New Orleans Price Current*, May 27, 1826.
[71] *New Orleans Price Current*, July 1, 1826.
[72] *Financial Register*, 1838, II, p. 410.

While therefore this was not a customary mode of carrying on the cotton trade, it was an entirely natural and reasonable proceeding for those who could afford to wait, or those who for any reason felt dissatisfied with their prospects in the local market. We find the practice continuing and perhaps should expect to find it increasing, as the planters became less dependent on the factor.[73]

SPECULATION IN COTTON BY THE BANKS

It has been mentioned earlier in this chapter that one of the methods of disposing of cotton was through the banks of the South. While it is not asserted that mercantile operations were ever characteristic of banking in the South, the history of the trading of the banks around the period of the panic of 1837 forms an interesting episode in the history of the cotton trade.

It is uncertain just what may have been the origin of the practice on the part of the banks of actually purchasing cotton from the planters and of making enormous advances to them. It probably was simply another manifestation of that spirit of speculation so prominent in the thirties and culminating in the crisis of 1837. But it was evidently very closely connected with the operations of Mr. Nicholas Biddle and his reorganised Bank of the United States.

A report on the Bank of the United States made in 1841 in the interests of the stockholders, gave a fairly clear idea of the operations of Mr. Biddle. The report stated:

"In the course of this investigation, the attention of the committee has been directed to certain accounts, which appear on the books as 'Advances on Merchandise,' but which were, in fact, payments for Cotton, Tobacco, and other produce, purchased by direction of the then President, Mr. Nicholas Biddle, and shipped to Europe on account of himself and others. . . .

"The first transactions were in July, 1837, and appear as advances to A. G. Jaudon, to purchase cotton for shipment to Baring, Brothers and Company, of Liverpool, the proceeds to be remitted to their house in London, then acting as agents of the Bank. The amount of these shipments was $3,182,988.28."[74]

[73] Cf. *Edinburgh Review*, vol. 127, No. 259, p. 273, January, 1868.

[74] Report on U. S. Bank, 1841, p. 18. The account of the operations of the Bank of the U. S. given in the text is drawn from this report, except as specifically noted in other footnotes.

In the autumn of 1837 a partnership between one of the directors of the bank, Mr. May Humphreys, and a son of Mr. Biddle was formed, under the name of Humphreys and Biddle. This house was established at Liverpool and from that time on it acted as the agent of the bank in the sale of all produce shipped to Liverpool by the bank.

The shipments of cotton were chiefly in the hands of a Philadelphia firm, Bevan and Humphreys. Their connection with Mr. Biddle is shown by the following letter:

"Philad. Oct. 19, 1837.

"Messrs. Bevan and Humphreys,
Gentlemen,

I may probably have occasion during the coming winter to direct some shipments of Cotton and other produce to the charge of our friends, Messrs. Humphreys and Biddle, of Liverpool. For greater convenience I propose to have the purchases made in the Southern States, by drafts which may be drawn upon you in consequence of credits opened for your house, to have the bills of lading forwarded to you to be transmitted to Messrs. H. and B. by you, that you should correspond with them in regard to the sales, and make such disposition of the proceeds as I may direct. . . .

N. Biddle."

This proposal was agreed to by Bevan and Humphreys, and shipments to a large amount were made to Biddle and Humphreys of Liverpool. The general scope of their operations is well illustrated by a statement given in a public letter on December 7, 1838, with reference to the claims of one John Ingersoll to be an agent of Humphreys and Biddle:

". . . Since then the undersigned have, at his repeated solicitation, but without even the knowledge of Messrs. Humphreys and Biddle, given him the general permission, extended to all shippers of cotton to the house, to draw upon them bills at sixty days' sight for two-thirds of the price, accompanied by bills of lading for the property actually shipped. . . .

Bevan and Humphreys."[75]

But a more active part was taken by Mr. Nicholas Biddle, for agents were appointed in the several Southern points, provided with letters of credit, and large purchases of cotton were made

---

[75] *Financial Register*, 1838, II, p. 380.

by them. Mr. Cabot, a member of the firm of Bevans and Humphreys, said of these purchases:

"At the time application was made to B. and H. to undertake this business, and for many months, it was firmly believed by me and them [the agents in Paris, etc.] that it was for the account and risk of the bank for the purpose of placing funds in Europe to provide for the large amount of Bonds which it was known became payable in the Spring of 1838."

Mr. Biddle indicated that the course pursued by his bank was much more high-minded than would be suggested by the account given above. Instead of using the bank's funds to purchase cotton for speculative purposes, it was intimated that advances were made to the planter to save him from the foreign purchaser. He said:

"In like manner the derangement of the currency placed the staples of the south entirely at the mercy of the foreign purchaser, who could have dictated the terms to the prostrated planter. It was thought proper to avert that evil by employing a large portion of the capital of the bank in making advances on southern produce."[76]

He also asserted that the funds were advanced to the merchants on the actual shipment of the produce to an American house in England, "willing and able to protect American property from the reckless waste with which it has been too often thrown into the market, with an entire disregard of American interests," and thus by implication denied speculation on the part of the bank itself.

The magnitude of operations in cotton of Mr. Biddle and his associates are seen from the following estimate of the stocks of cotton held in Liverpool:

"The agents of the United States bank here, Humphreys and Biddle, have an immense stock on hand and are daily receiving more. . . . The principal holders of cotton here at present are as follows:

Humphreys and Biddle, about	125,000 bales
Brown and Company . . .	120,000
Baring Brothers	55,000
Denniston	50,000

"The whole stock on hand . . . some say it reaches 500,000 bales. The Browns are the principal sellers—the other houses holding on as much

[76] *Financial Register*, 1838, II, p. 393.

as possible. Hereafter the American trade in cotton will be controlled by the three B's; the Biddles, the Barings, and the Browns. The day of the three W's is past and gone forever."[77]

The transactions continued during the years 1837, 1838, and 1839, and amounted to about nine million dollars. Unfortunately for Mr. Biddle and for the bank, the last shipments were unprofitable, occasioning a loss of about $960,000. This loss was settled by Mr. Biddle and some of the others in the concern who were directly responsible for the policy pursued.

But speculation in cotton was not confined at this period to the Bank of the United States. The fever seems to have afflicted many of the Southern banks. A news item from New Orleans in 1838 stated that the Mississippi banks, after having gone headlong into cotton, turned their attention towards provisions, and bought up nearly all the pork in the city, "and their purchases in Cincinnati and other places have been on a monopolising or forestalling scale; the article in consequence, has advanced $6 per bbl."[78] Another notice of purchases by the banks ran as follows:

"A letter from Natchez [Miss.], under date of the 13th Dec. says,— 'Business is dull yet. The banks are still buying cotton at 12½ cents. Many northerners are here waiting their withdrawal, to invest for remittances.' "[79]

An investigation, conducted by the State Bank Examiners of Mississippi, into the affairs of the Mississippi and Alabama Railroad and Banking Company, 1838, showed that that bank had invested over $350,000 in cotton, and had a total of about 60,000 bales, purchased and shipped on account of planters and others, with Humphreys and Biddle in Liverpool. Against this the bank had drawn bills to the amount of over a million dollars. The bank had established agencies at several points on the Mississippi, Yazoo, and Pearl rivers, which were supplied with funds to advance on cotton delivered.[80]

A statement by the examiners to the effect that there were in Mississippi upwards of forty incorporated banks and branches,

77 *Financial Register*, 1838, II, p. 140. Liverpool report of July 10, 1838.
78 *Ibid.*, p. 29.
79 *Ibid.*, 1837, I, p. 237.
80 *Ibid.*, 1838, II, pp. 265-268.

all endowed with privileges similar to those of the above-mentioned bank, shows the possible extent of the mercantile operations by banks.[81]

It is doubtful whether this practice was continued by the majority of the banks. There seems to be little mention of it after 1839, and probably losses, and the sobering effects of the panic of 1837 brought most of the banks to their senses. There was, of course, and still is, a most legitimate place for the banks in the financing of the cotton exports; but purchasing for its own account is not a proper function of a bank, nor is it wise policy to tie up all the funds of a bank in any one article.

SUMMARY

We find the planters dealing with the outside world largely through the numerous and important class of factors. The factors performed in general three services; (1) they acted as selling agents of cotton; (2) they acted as buying agents of plantation and personal supplies; and, (3) they supplied the planter with funds and credit by means of which he kept his plantation going during the growing season.

The factors dealt with other factors, who might act on their own behalf, or as agents for Northern or foreign mercantile or manufacturing firms in the purchase of cotton; or they dealt with the agents of such firms sent directly to the South to purchase the cotton. In all probability the most numerous class of buyers were the commission houses located in the South and acting as agents for American or European concerns located in New York.

So far as can be observed, there was very little change in the method of handling cotton in the South during the period under consideration. The only development which is apparent was a tendency for the cotton to be purchased more and more on British account, and for less to be shipped abroad by the American owner to be sold on a commission basis. This feature has already been discussed in Chapter III.

The radical changes that occurred in the cotton trade in America did not manifest themselves until after the Civil War, and are therefore not properly a subject of discussion in this study.

81 *Financial Register*, 1838, II, p. 267.

CHAPTER V

THE TRADE IN BRITISH MANUFACTURES,
1800-1815

IT is true that in this period a relatively large volume of imports was brought into the United States from China, India, the East Indies, and other countries by the shipowning merchants of the Eastern seaboard ports in a way essentially different from that pursued in the trade with Great Britain. In many respects this trade is the more interesting; there is more of color, of the romantic and adventurous, attached to it. The more prosaic and regular commerce with Great Britain and with the countries of Europe gives us, however, the beginnings of the methods at present in use in foreign commerce, and shows more clearly the changes effected in the ways of handling goods in foreign trade by the revolutionary developments in the technique of production and of transportation.

A complete survey of this phase of foreign trade would involve a tracing of all the steps in the progress of the goods from the manufacturer in Great Britain to the consumer in the United States. In this study, however, we shall content ourselves with following the goods from the manufacturer through various agencies until they reach the American importer or wholesale merchant, and shall treat of the domestic marketing methods of Great Britain and the United States only incidentally.

There were three agents of greatest importance in this trade—the British merchant, the British manufacturer, and the American merchant. The relations of these three, one to the other, at any one time, gave to the organisation its distinctive tone. Conceivably any one of the three might have been the dominant figure in the foreign trade of the two countries, supplying the initiative, assuming the risks of trade, and generally directing the goods from England to America. Our task is to determine the relative importance of these three agents, to note the changes in their relative positions, and, so far as is possible, to account for such changes.

In the attempt to arrive at a solution of the problem as stated, it is convenient to divide the period under consideration into three parts: (a) from 1800 to 1815; (b) from 1815 to 1830; and (c) from 1830 to 1850. In the first period we find the British merchant the outstanding figure; he received orders from America for goods, and he himself also assumed the risks of commerce by sending out goods on consignment to his agents and correspondents in America. In the second period the position of the British manufacturer attracts our attention, for he seems to have been forced into marketing his own goods because of the inability or the unwillingness of the merchant to purchase his entire output. And in the third period the American merchant became a much more important factor in the foreign commerce than he had been previously.

The sections that follow will be devoted largely to proving the dominance of the particular agent in the period indicated, and the attention of the reader will therefore be directed to the operations of one or another of these agents, to the apparent neglect of the other agents. It should be realised clearly at the outset, however, that in no period does one particular agent alone handle the marketing of British manufactured goods; we find all three agents in existence and functioning throughout the first half of the nineteenth century. The manufacturer marketed a part of his output in the first period, when the British merchant was the most important merchandising agent; and, similarly, in the last period—from 1830 to 1850—when the chief topic of interest was the growing importance of the American merchant, the British manufacturer and merchant were vital factors in the distributive system.

TRADE ORGANISATION

The Position of the British Merchant. In the period from 1800 until the beginning of the War of 1812, most of the goods exported from Great Britain to the United States were purchased in Great Britain by the British or the American merchant and exported on the account of and at the risk of the merchant. The manufacturer, as an independent exporter of his own goods, was of minor importance.

For evidence in the study of this particular problem we rely to a large extent on the two reports of Parliamentary committees on the effects of the Orders in Council on the American trade.

Direct testimony was given in these reports (one in 1808, the other in 1812) by manufacturers in various lines as to the way in which they disposed of their goods. Very few of the manufacturers stated that they sold their goods directly to the foreign houses abroad. The weight of the evidence seemed to show that the manufacturer as a general rule sold to merchants in Great Britain, who attended to the shipment of the goods to America.

Greenwood, a woolen manufacturer, stated that he usually did not export his goods: "We have sometimes exported to America a little; we have generally sold our goods finished to the American merchants here.[1] Broom, a manufacturer of carpets, did not deal directly with the American market, but through merchants in London.[2] Milward, a maker of spoons, received his orders from the merchants of Birmingham, engaged in the American trade.[3] Illidge, a tinplate worker, stated that he never exported to America on his own account, but that all his goods were sold to merchants, principally at Birmingham.[4] Cook, a manufacturer of jewelry, stated: "I have not been in the habit of exporting goods to America; I export my goods through the hands of the merchants at Birmingham, . . ."[5] Webster, a wire manufacturer, was asked if he received orders from American correspondents. He replied that all his orders came to him from merchants in the town of Birmingham.[6] Kay, a manufacturer of cotton and woolen textiles, asserted that he was not an exporter, but a manufacturer, and generally sold to merchants.[7] Ryland, manufacturing coach-harness and saddlery furniture, said that "we trade with the merchants on this side of the water, and they export the goods to their correspondents in the United States."[8] Mr. Atwood, a banker of Birmingham, made a more general statement in regard to the practices in the export of Birmingham wares:

". . . I never yet knew any Birmingham goods exported to any great amount by any individual, except Birmingham merchants; I have known very large amounts of Birmingham goods sent by Bir-

[1] Parl. Papers, Report on Orders in Council, 1812, p. 128.
[2] *Ibid.*, p. 122.
[3] *Ibid.*, p. 110.
[4] *Ibid.*, p. 93.
[5] *Ibid.*, p. 91.
[6] *Ibid.*, p. 80.
[7] *Ibid.*, pp. 218, 219.
[8] *Ibid.*, p. 49.

mingham factors to Glasgow, and to Bristol, and to Edinburgh, which I have understood have been shipped principally to the United States of America by Glasgow merchants."[9]

The importance of merchants in the export of Sheffield wares was brought out by the testimony of Mr. Bailey, an exporting merchant. He was asked the number of manufacturers exclusively engaged on work for the American market, and replied that he was unable to give a definite answer, but stated that there were eighteen mercantile houses exporting solely to America, as contrasted with nine export houses dealing with the other foreign markets.[10]

The testimony of merchants of a later period on the practices prevalent before 1815 supports our conclusion—that the merchant was then the dominant figure in the export trade—and is perhaps more valuable, as the early methods stood out, in the minds of those testifying, in sharp contrast to those in use at the later period when the evidence was taken. The following quotation, taken from evidence given in 1834, refers particularly to the practices of the merchants and manufacturers of Glasgow before 1815, but is an important indication of the general practices.

"The change of doing foreign business in Glasgow, especially since the year 1816, but more especially since 1826, is this; previous to that the manufacturer was in the way of selling his goods to the merchant; the merchant bought his goods according to his orders, and sent them to his foreign house; but, especially since 1826 it has been the custom for the manufacturer to consign his goods to an agent abroad; . . ."[11]

Another witness referred to the "injudicious mode by which foreign markets are supplied to a great extent by the manufacturers of Glasgow of late years; that is, by consignments on the part of the manufacturers of these goods themselves, instead of their being supplied as they were originally, by merchants having located establishments in foreign countries."[12]

A witness, who testified in 1833 on the practice then prevalent of consignments by manufacturers directly to the foreign markets, stated:

"First of all they [the manufacturers] are driven to make shipments; formerly manufacturers would never ship if they could sell

9 Parl. Papers, Report on Orders in Council, 1812, p. 17.
10 *Ibid.*, p. 132.
11 Parl. Papers, Report on Hand-Loom Weavers, 1834, p. 100.
12 *Ibid.*, p. 163.

their goods at a profit; but when a stagnation takes place, which it did a few years ago, they then prefer to try the market themselves, and to take both the profit of the merchant and of the manufacturer."[13]

And again, showing that the manufacturer had been forced to turn merchant after 1815, a manufacturer in 1834 spoke with regret of the old days when the merchant sought out the manufacturer. Now, he said, with the present glut of goods the manufacturer has to seek the merchant, rather than the merchant seeking the manufacturer.[14]

The Relation of the Merchant to the British Market. Shipments of goods to America took place at two different periods of the year. There were the spring shipments, from the middle of January until the middle of April, and the fall shipments, during the months of July and August. As it generally took from a month to six weeks to manufacture the goods and prepare them for shipment, merchants, who purchased from the manufacturers, were required to place their orders for goods fairly early.[15]

It is not clear to what extent the merchants secured the goods for export by placing definite orders with the manufacturers, and to what extent they relied on the regular supplies in the market. Of the manufacturers mentioned above, Broom, Milward, Illidge, and Webster were the only ones who spoke of having received orders from merchants, but it was in all probability a general custom, the extent of which at any particular time depended on the general state of demand in the market.

Some of the merchants made purchases in the various cloth halls which existed in different cities. Of this practice an early report (1806) on the woolen manufacture said:

"In fact there are many Merchants of very large capital and of the highest credit who for several generations have gone on purchasing in the Halls. . . ."[16]

John Oxley, a woolen merchant, purchased largely at these cloth halls,[17] and somewhat later, Mr. Gott, a cloth manufacturer

---

[13] Parl. Papers, Report on Manufactures, 1833, p. 297.
[14] Parl. Papers, Report on Hand-Loom Weavers, 1834, p. 610.
[15] Parl. Papers, Evidence of Merchants, 1808, pp. 2, 80.
[16] Parl. Papers, Report on Woolen Manufacture, 1806 (268), p. 11.
[17] *Ibid.*, (Evidence) 1806 (268a), p. 173.

and export merchant at Leeds, testified that he secured cloth for export in the White Cloth Hall at Leeds.[18]

But a great quantity of textiles and other goods was purchased from agents of the manufacturer, in London, Manchester, and other important commercial cities. Broom, the carpet manufacturer alluded to above, sold his carpets to merchants through an agent in London. James Hunter testified in 1818 that for more than twenty-five years he had been the London agent for the sale of cotton goods, for and on account of manufacturers. His business was with exporters only, and the average yearly sales which he negotiated amounted to more than £500,000.[19] And it seems to have been a fairly general custom for Manchester goods to be sold through agents. Mr. Joshua Bates, who was examined in 1833, gave evidence to the effect that it had long been the practice for agents of the manufacturers in London and Manchester to arrange for the sale of the goods, but that by 1833 the agencies in London had been done away with, because of the greater accessibility of Manchester.[20]

Even before 1800 we find goods sold in London by agents of the manufacturers. In 1744 it was noted that linens were consigned to factors in London, who advanced money on them to the manufacturers.

"Mr. Hollyor . . . added, That the discouragement to the Manufacturer was the greater, in regard that it was customary for the Factors

---

[18] Parl. Papers, Report on British Wool Trade, 1828 (515), VIII, p. 281.
Of the relation of the merchants to the cloth halls, Clapham says: "Formerly there existed an important class of specialized merchants, woollen merchants or worsted merchants as the case might be, in the manufacturing districts—above all in Yorkshire—through whose hands all the goods passed, whether they were intended for the home or the foreign trade. This mercantile class was absolutely indispensable, so long as a large part of the manufacturing was carried on by the small master clothiers; for the clothiers laid no claim to commercial knowledge. They sold their goods to the merchants in the cloth halls of Halifax, Huddersfield, Bradford, and Leeds, buildings erected at various dates in the 18th century for the convenience of the trade. . . . With the decline of the small clothiers the cloth hall business slackened. This was first noticeable in the worsted trade. Dealings in the cloth hall at Bradford came to an end in the early '50's; they lasted longer at Huddersfield, while at Leeds they continued far into the last quarter of the nineteenth century." Clapham, *Woollen and Worsted Industries*, 1907, p. 162.
[19] Parl. Papers, Report on Duties on Cotton Prints, 1818, III, p. 32.
[20] Parl. Papers, Report on Manufactures, 1833, p. 61.

in London to advance money to the Manufacturer on their sending their goods to London; for which the Manufacturer paid Interest to the Factors during all the Time their Goods lay unsold."[21]

James stated that in 1775 there were in London a large number of cloth and stuff merchants who either purchased goods on their own account, or acted as commission merchants for the merchants and manufacturers of Norwich, Sudbury, Coventry, and the North of England. Some of these merchants went periodically to the cloth and stuff manufacturing districts to purchase their stocks.[22]

Relations of the British Merchant to the American Market. There were probably some merchants who confined themselves to the safer and less speculative business of shipping only on the receipt of orders from America. John Bainbridge, a merchant trading both to the Continent and to America, received orders from his correspondents, and these formed the basis of his business.[23] William Bell testified that he never shipped to America on his own account, but always executed orders.[24]

Most merchants, however, received orders from their American agents or correspondents, and also shipped goods to America which had not been ordered, but which they felt could be sold there at a profit. Martin, a shipping merchant, claimed that when he exported goods from England it was "on account of the American merchant in America and on account of the British merchant or manufacturer resident in this country."[25] Another merchant was asked if it were the custom of the house of which he was a member to send shipments to America for a market, or to send only such goods as had been ordered by the American merchant. He replied that occasionally it was customary to do both.[26]

The relative importance of shipments of goods in response to orders from America and of consignments sent at the risk of the British merchant can be determined with a fair degree of

---

[21] Parl. Papers, Reports from Committee, 1st Series, 1744, vol. II, p. 69, Report on Linen Trade.

[22] James, *"History of Worsted Manufacture in England,* 1857, p. 274, note.

[23] Parl. Papers, Evidence of Merchants, 1808, p. 121.

[24] *Ibid.*, p. 35.

[25] *Ibid.*, p. 48.

[26] *Ibid.*, p. 6.

accuracy. That shipments made on order were fairly large in amount is unquestionable; indeed, certain evidence would lead us to think them of major significance. Mr. Thornely, testifying in 1812, seemed of this opinion. His testimony follows:

"Are not the exports to the United States more on American account than on British? I believe they are partly on British, but chiefly on American."[27]

Bainbridge was questioned in 1808 as to the practice of his own house in the American trade, and stated that it seldom happened that his house assumed any risk in exporting goods.

"Do you send goods to America generally on your own account, or on account of persons residing there? Solely on account of persons residing in America; we have never been in the habit of shipping goods on our own account from the time of the commencement of the house, which is nearly forty years; since the commencement of the war we have not shipped on our own account, unless it happened to be any article remaining in our stores."[28]

John Oxley, a cloth and blanket merchant, claimed that two-thirds of his business was with the American trade in Great Britain, the other third with houses in America. By the American trade in Great Britain he meant houses in London, Liverpool, and Glasgow that dealt with merchants in America. He was asked if these houses dealt with America in consequence of orders received from American merchants, and averred that they did.[29] And finally, it was stated in an article in the *Edinburgh Review* in 1837 that "the export of British manufactures to the United States was formerly effected by English houses executing orders for the Americans. . . ."[30]

But the most illuminating information regarding the customs of the trade, and the extent to which exports were made on British and on American account, is given in the testimony of Mr. T. Martin in the Parliamentary investigation of 1808.

Martin was in business as a shipper of goods and as a commission merchant. As a shipper he simply handled the details of packing and transportation, and received for this service a commission; as a commission merchant he received consignments

27 Parl. Papers, Report on Orders in Council, 1812, p. 355.
28 Parl. Papers, Evidence of Merchants, 1808, p. 121.
29 *Ibid.*, p. 85.
30 *Edinburgh Review*, 1837, vol. LXV, §132, p. 229.

of produce from America, and executed orders given him by his American correspondents. He was therefore in a position to know quite accurately the prevailing methods. His statements are clear and unequivocal. He believed that the great mass of goods sent from Great Britain to America was sent on British account, and that the amount shipped on American account in consequence of orders given, or because of purchases by Americans in Great Britain, was insignificant.

"Do you suppose that the great mass of exports are principally sent out on British account or on American account? On British account, certainly, the great mass."

"Is not also a considerable proportion sent out on American account? I should call it an inconsiderable proportion when compared with the great mass."

"In general the goods shipped from Liverpool is in consequence of orders coming from America? I must explain that business; it was by no means in general from orders from America, they are principally shipped by Merchants in this Country to America."

"Without any previous orders from America? Certainly, because it is on their own account they are guided by the prospect of different circumstances, which induce them to ship or not to ship; they cannot be said to receive orders for the shipment of goods, for the quantity of goods exported for orders is small in proportion to the goods shipped by the British merchant on his own account."[31]

Branch Houses in America. When the goods were ordered or purchased by the American merchant they were shipped to his house in the United States and disposed of by him in the ordinary manner. Goods shipped by British merchants on their own account were consigned either to their own agents or branch houses in America, or to American commission houses for sale on a commission basis.

We have already seen in many of the passages cited that the presence of agents or branch houses is tacitly assumed, and there are many specific references on the part of individual merchants to agents in the United States. Jaffrey, a London merchant in the American trade, received orders from his house in New York, which was in the charge of his partner.[32] The firm of Nathaniel and Falkener Phillips and Company, of Manchester, kept an agent in America. He was an Englishman, and was paid a regu-

31 Parl. Papers, Evidence of Merchants, 1808, pp. 49-50.
32 Parl. Papers, Report on Orders in Council, 1812, p. 339.

lar salary, and not paid on a commission basis.[33] Rideout, an exporter of Birmingham wares, mentioned that his partner was in America for the purpose of selling goods.[34] Scholefield, another Birmingham merchant, dealing in brass, iron, and steel, had an "agent resident" in America.[35] Wiggin, a general exporter in the American trade, and exporting almost entirely on his own and his partner's account, said that he had two brothers in America looking out for his business interests.[36] Thomas Kinder, a merchant, maintained two establishments, one in London and the other in New York.[37] A Glasgow manufacturer, speaking in 1834 of the conditions of trade before 1816, remarked that it had been the custom for the merchant to buy his goods according to his orders, and send them to his foreign house.[38]

The existence in America of agents and branch houses of British mercantile firms is easily demonstrated, but it seems quite impossible to secure accurate data as to the universality of the practice. Doubtless only the more important firms in the Anglo-American trade would find such an arrangement profitable; others contented themselves with the services of American commission houses.

The American Importing Merchant. It is of course a matter of general knowledge that for centuries foreign merchants had come to England to purchase goods for shipment to their respective countries. Their presence in 1814 was noted by an anonymous writer who spoke of the "foreign merchants, having concerns and dealings in British commodities in their own countries and residing in this to transact the mercantile business connected with them."[39] James, a cotton spinner and manufacturer of plain and figured cambrics, stated in 1818 that he sold chiefly to the "foreign buyer."[40] And we know that of these foreign merchants or buyers many were Americans.

The evidence of the witnesses before the committees of 1808 and 1812 shows quite clearly that at those dates there were a number of American merchants resident in Great Britain, who

[33] Parl. Papers, Report on Orders in Council, 1812, p. 435.
[34] *Ibid.*, p. 67.
[35] *Ibid.*, p. 99.
[36] *Ibid.*, p. 324.
[37] *Ibid.*, p. 450.
[38] Parl. Papers, Report on Hand-Loom Weavers, 1834, p. 100.
[39] *An Essay on . . . Trade*, 1814, p. 44.
[40] Parl. Papers, Report on Printed Cotton Goods, 1818, III (279), p. 37.

were purchasing on their own account either from the manufacturers, or from the British merchants. William Rathbone, a shipping merchant, who held large stocks of goods in his warehouses belonging to American merchants, was asked if upon the repeal of the Orders in Council he would ship those goods with or without insurance. He answered that as many of the owners of the goods were then in England he would look to them for the necessary orders.[41] Whitehouse, a nail ironmonger, spoke of a "gentleman from Boston, of one of the most respectable importing houses there, who is in this country," who had given him an order for hardware.[42] We have, further, an account of the activities of the firm of John Guest and Company, both the partners of which were Americans. It was the custom for one of the partners to reside in America and the other in London, the London partner executing orders sent him by the partner in America.[43] Charles Everett was an American commission merchant in business in Liverpool. He stated in 1821 that there were a number of similar merchants located there, buying on their own account or selecting goods for the account of merchants of America.[44]

A certain portion of the trade hence was in the hands of American merchants, who came to England to buy goods. Bates said, in 1833, that Americans had always made purchases in person from the British manufacturers and merchants.[45] But it does not seem to have been the prevailing mode; the British merchant was more important both as a purchaser of goods on American account and as a purchaser of goods on his own account, which he consigned to America on his own responsibility.

The Manufacturers as Merchants. It is quite noticeable throughout this period, and indeed before 1800, that there was a transfer of capital from the mercantile pursuits to manufacturing, and in some cases from manufacturing to merchandising. There seems to have been a class of capitalists who combined manufacturing and merchandising, and who received the name of "merchant manufacturers." James, in speaking of the manufacturers in the worsted trade in the latter part of the eighteenth

---

41 Parl. Papers, Report on Orders in Council, 1812, p. 430.
42 *Ibid.*, p. 22.
43 Parl. Papers, Evidence of Merchants, 1808, pp. 16-18.
44 Parl. Papers, Report on Foreign Trade, 1821, VI (746), pp. 341-343.
45 Parl. Papers, Report on Manufactures, 1833, p. 61.

century, noted that they were merchants as well as manufacturers.

> " 'They were merchants as well as manufacturers, and traded to the Baltic, Germany, Holland, Spain, and Portugal, and through them to the great markets of Brazil and South America, then at the acme of their glory; to Italy and to China by the India Company.' "[46]

Another early writer complained that

> "Thus, manufacturers and tradesmen having gained a capital by supplying merchants, commence shipping their own goods; and besides becoming independent of the merchant, occasion his commission to become burthensome; . . ."[47]

But the movement was not only from the manufacturing to the mercantile lines; it ran in the other direction also. In a report of 1806 on the state of the woolen trade in Great Britain, it was stated that many merchants had established woolen factories, but "were not greatly attached to that system, but persisted in it only because their Buildings and Machinery must otherwise lie a dead weight upon their hands."[48]

Clapham notes that while in Yorkshire the merchant was an indispensable medium for the disposal of woolens and worsteds because of the large number of small clothiers, in the West of England, where the number of small manufacturers was small even in the eighteenth century, the relation between manufacturer and merchant was of a different character.

> "Many of those who controlled the industrial operations were in the first instance merchants who bought wool, had it spun, woven, dyed, and finished, and then sold the pieces. That is to say, the industrial organisation was capitalistic before the factory age began, and the industrial and commercial organisations were not quite clearly separated from one another; though clothiers not infrequently sold to merchants, particularly to London merchants."[49]

This process of transferring capital to manufacturing was not confined to the period before 1815, but was fairly prominent

---

[46] James, *History of Worsted Manufacture*, 1857, p. 261. Quoted from the *East Anglian Newspaper*, of February 7, 1832.

[47] *An Essay on . . . Trade*, 1814, p. 8.

[48] Parl. Papers, Report on Woolen Manufacture, 1806 (268), p. 11.

[49] Clapham, *Woollen and Worsted Industries* (1907), p. 163.

after that date as well. A witness in 1828 said that the domestic manufacturers used to have the whole trade and sell to the merchants, who had become manufacturers, and manufacturers on a large scale, and complained that the change had made it difficult for the domestic manufacturer to dispose of his product profitably.[50] A wool stapler, called before the same committee, was asked if the manufacturers, by stapling their wool of late years more than they used to, had deprived him of his trade, and replied that his business had suffered in so far as there were ''a great many more merchant manufacturers than there used to be.''[51]

Concrete evidence of transfer of capital to manufacturing is afforded in the following evidence of a merchant-manufacturer, taken in 1824. The committee asked him if he were not in the shipping business, and he replied:

". . . we are [shipping merchants] still; the manufacturing is only a branch of our business; we have houses abroad, and we put up the works for the purpose of supplying our foreign houses."[52]

With respect to the cotton trade and the general tendency towards integration of the various branches of that trade, including the marketing, the following statement is very significant.

"While spinning was a good trade, those who spun their own materials constantly undersold the manufacturer who had to buy his yarns. This trade is now taken up by spinners generally; either the spinner has become a manufacturer in addition to spinning, or the manufacturer has become a spinner in addition to a manufacturer . . . and both have become merchants in some cases."[53]

This general confusion of the functions of the manufacturer and the merchant make it difficult to generalise on the importance of the manufacturer as the distributor of his goods to the foreign trade. We know in a general way from the evidence cited above that he did market his own goods, and the testimony of manufacturers of 1808 and 1812 showed that some exported directly. Leach, a manufacturer of stockings, asserted

---

50 Parl. Papers, Report on British Wool Trade, 1828, VIII (515), p. 258.
51 *Ibid.*, p. 135.
52 Parl. Papers, Report on Manufactures, 1833, p. 329.
53 *Ibid.*, p. 559.

that he had received many orders from America, and also that he shipped to America on his own account.[54] Weight, a Manchester manufacturer, when asked if he ever traded as a merchant in the market, stated that he bought very considerably from various manufacturers, "indeed very extensively. . . ."[55] Another instance of the direct connection of the British manufacturer and the American merchant is afforded by the testimony of William Brown, a shipping merchant of Liverpool. He stated in 1812 that he had in his warehouses merchandise of various kinds valued at about £100,000, and awaiting the repeal of the Orders in Council, to be shipped to America. When questioned about the ownership of them he said that many of them belonged to merchants in America who had sent the orders directly to the manufacturers.[56] McKerrel, a cotton manufacturer and merchant, sold his own goods, and, in fact, had established sales agencies abroad for that purpose.[57]

While there is, therefore, evidence to show that American merchants sent orders directly to the manufacturer, or that the manufacturer perhaps solicited orders from the American merchants, and that in one or two cases the manufacturer had his own foreign sales agencies to which he made consignments, there is no evidence forthcoming to lead us to believe that the manufacturer made a practice of consigning his goods directly to commission houses or other agents in America to be sold for what they could bring. On the contrary, the evidence which we have indicates that when consignments on speculation were made, they were, as a general rule, at the risk of merchants, and not of the manufacturers. Hence we conclude that the manufacturer in this period was of minor importance as an agent in the export trade organisation.

54 Parl. Papers, Report on Orders in Council, 1812, p. 179.
55 *Ibid.*, p. 277.
56 *Ibid.*, pp. 294-295.
57 *Ibid.*, p. 521. McKerrel's evidence follows:

"In what branch of business is your mercantile house concerned? Our mercantile house depends principally upon the sale of our manufactures; and the sale of other manufactures of the same species, of other manufacturers; we are principally confined to the cotton line.

"To what part of the world do you trade? Previous to the war we had correspondents in every part of Europe with the exception of the Austrian dominions, and Norway."

CREDIT RELATIONS

Throughout the first half of the nineteenth century we should expect to find the merchants and bankers of Great Britain extending credit for long periods to the American merchants. The supply of American capital was limited, the needs of the people growing, and the nature of the occupation of a majority of the American people such as to make it necessary for someone to extend credit to them.

Goods of all sorts were generally sold by the merchants in the United States on credit. The author of *Trade and Commerce of New York* stated that previous to 1812 the country dealers generally purchased goods from the city merchants on a credit of six months. A common condition was that the country merchant should make payments from time to time as he was able, paying interest on that amount which remained unpaid at the end of six months; but he was considered as liable for the whole debt at the expiration of the fixed time of credit.[58] This meant, of course, that the credit was for considerably more than six months. Clarke says of the credit extensions:

"Long credits characterised business operations. Cash transactions were so rare as to be negligible. In the South terms of payment usually ran from crop to crop, and even in the North they approximated this period. Almy and Brown sold yarn from the Slater mills on three to nine months' payment, according to the individual standing and importance of creditors."[59]

Callender stated that down to 1857 it was the common practice for merchants in the seaboard cities to sell to the merchants of the interior upon eight and ten months' credit.[60]

A different view of the time which was allowed for payment was given by a writer in 1843. He was inveighing against the long credits given at that time by the New Englanders to merchants.

"Now, what was the course of things thirty or forty years ago, and down to a late period? Why, with half or perhaps a third of the capital among the class of persons who are ready to stand between the im-

[58] *Trade and Commerce of New York*, 1820, p. 28.
[59] Clarke, *History of Manufactures*, 1916, p. 365.
[60] Callender, G. S., English Capital and American Resources, 1897, pp. 38-39. (MSS. in Harvard College Library.)

porter and manufacturers of goods and the consumers of goods, there was no difficulty in finding buyers at two, three, and four months' credit in all our commercial cities."[61]

It is believed that this is a somewhat colored view of the situation; for there appears to be no other evidence to substantiate this statement.

Since the importing merchants as well as the wholesale merchants of the United States found it necessary to extend credit to their customers, they in turn were forced to a large extent to rely on the credit facilities offered by the British houses with which they traded. The accumulated capital of Great Britain enabled her merchants to undertake this better and more cheaply than the merchants of any other land, and it was so general a custom that M. Talleyrand maintained that it was really Great Britain who carried on the trade of America.

"De plus, les grands capitaux des négociants Anglais leur permettent d'accorder des crédits plus long qu'aucun negociant d'aucune autre nation ne le pourroit faire; ces crédits sont au moins d'un an, et souvent de plus. Il en résulte que le négociant Américain qui tire ses marchandises d'Angleterre, n'emploie presque aucun capital à lui dans le commerce, et le fait presque tout entier sur les capitaux Anglais. C'est donc réellement l'Angleterre qui fait le commerce de consommation de l'Amérique."[62]

In considering M. Talleyrand's general view of the credit relations of America and Great Britain, the *Edinburgh Review* remarked that the long credits extended to the Americans were in reality forced upon the British merchants, and were the means by which they maintained their hold on the American trade.

"So far, then, from the English merchants repaying themselves for this long credit which they give their American customers, this credit, unrecompensed, is the cause of their capital finding employment in the American states, and the consequences of that capital being voluntary on the part of the creditor; an accommodation which he allows his debtor for a certain consideration. On the contrary it is a matter of necessity and is forced upon him by the competition of other capitalists, while it is rendered practicable by the great extent of his own stock."[63]

[61] Lee, *Letters,* p. 52.
[62] Talleyrand, *Mémoire,* 1805, p. 19.
[63] *Edinburgh Review,* 1805, vol. VI, p. 75.

The testimony of the merchants of the period was practically unanimous on the subject of the length of the credits granted to American houses purchasing British manufactured goods. The two reports of Parliamentary committees in 1808 and 1812, so often cited above, give us abundant evidence on this point.

Mr. Wood, a merchant and manufacturer of Manchester, was questioned on the credit terms which his house (Thomas Phillips and Company) gave.

"Can you state to the House the usual period of credit at which goods are sold and exported to America, by your house? The nominal credit is twelve months.

"What may be the average period for which credit is given? I conceive that my house does not receive its remittances from America, on the average, at less than eighteen months.

"What do you conceive to be the shortest credit in your line of business? A credit of six months.

". . . If I estimate the shorter credit at about one third of the total business done to America, I conceive it is a very large allowance."[64]

Mr. Wood thought that possibly the time allowed for payment by his house was somewhat longer than would be general in the American trade, and estimated the average credit in the export trade to America to be not less than fifteen months.[65]

Jeremiah Naylor, a woolen merchant, and one of the largest in the trade (according to his statement), asserted that the credit which he usually gave to the American merchants was twelve months, but that often he was required to extend the period of payment.[66] He noted also that as long a credit was given to the British houses with connections in America.[67] Mr. Phillips, of the house of N. and F. Phillips and Company, chiefly engaged in the export of cotton goods to the United States, stated that "upon the average it is eighteen months before we receive a return for

[64] Parl. Papers, Evidence of Merchants, 1808, p. 2.

[65] *Ibid.*, p. 2.

[66] Wood noted in connection with this point that the Americans frequently exceeded the term of credit: "it is usual in the American trade for the English exporter to charge interest to his American debtor from the expiration of the credit; this interest is regularly allowed by the American debtor, and he does not consider it any great reflection on his character for punctuality if he is occasionally a few months in arrears for his payments." Parl. Papers, Evidence of Merchants, 1808, pp. 2-3.

[67] *Account of Merchants in Wool and Woollen Trade of Great Britain,* 1800, pp. 135-136.

the value we export,'' but thought that the average period of credit given by the trade in Manchester was not quite so long—probably between twelve and fifteen months—thus supporting the estimate made by Wood.[68] William Bell, another merchant of the same period, asserted that he gave a credit of twelve months, but that usually eighteen months elapsed before he received payment.[69]

All goods were not, however, sold on long-time payments. Some of the American merchants were in a position to pay cash, or to settle in a shorter time than would be willingly granted. Potts, an exporter of Birmingham wares to America, stated that in many cases the Americans preferred to pay cash.

"In a great many instances, they preferred paying ready money and taking the discount, remitting on what we call the arrival."[70]

Stephen Girard, in a letter to Baring Brothers of London, wrote that

"My commercial capital enables me to sell my goods on credit, and to carry on my maritime business throughout, cash in Hand, without the aid of discount. All this I owe principally to my close attention to business and to the resources which this fine country affords to all active or industrious men."[71]

A merchant who acted as a shipper for British firms and as a commission merchant for American merchants, claimed that he frequently purchased goods on American account, paying for them in cash. "Having the proceeds in our hands we purchase them for prompt payment, on account of the advantage which it gives to the person for whom they are purchased." But that the volume of goods thus purchased for cash was small is evidenced by the following testimony of the same merchant:

"That [purchases for cash] is then a case in which you have before had proceeds in hand, arising from antecedent remittances? Certainly; but that is to a very small amount; indeed, compared with the quantity of goods sent out to America from this Country, it does take place to a degree, but to a very small one, when compared with the bulk of goods sent out.

68 Parl. Papers, Evidence of Merchants, 1808, p. 9.
69 *Ibid.*, p. 35.
70 Parl. Papers, Report on Orders in Council, 1812, p. 30.
71 McMaster, *Life and Times of Stephen Girard* (1918), II, p. 307.

"Are the rest sent out on credit? The bulk of goods sent out are on credit.

"What length of credit, when they are sent out on credit, is given? Twelve and eighteen months is the usual credit (so far as I have had any information upon the subject) given by manufacturers."[72]

On goods bought by the British merchant from the manufacturer, the term of credit was possibly not so long, yet the bills given the manufacturer in payment for goods ran from three to nine months, and even longer. A witness, speaking of the credit in Glasgow in 1811 said:

"The usual date of bills given by the Merchant to the Manufacturer is six or nine months, but in some cases it may be extended to twelve months; in cases where the goods are sold by an agent in London, that agent interposes his credit, and gives an accommodation to the Manufacturer sooner, if he requires it, taking his chance of payment from the Merchant."[73]

The tenor of the bills drawn in Lancashire and London against purchases was apparently shorter than in Glasgow. Samuel Guerney, one of the largest of the bill brokers, stated that:

"We discount bills which have two or three years to run sometimes; there are very long bills drawn in particular lines, but we do not often discount bills which have longer than a year to run; in some trades they draw regularly at twelve months; in others at six, in others at nine, in others at three and four; the bank of England never discounts beyond sixty-five days."[74]

Another witness, a Liverpool merchant, gave the following testimony, tending to show that the usual interval between sale of goods and time of receiving payment in cash was about six months.

"The practice in Liverpool by which all goods are bot and sold is that at the expiration of a given credit of from ten days to three months as may be agreed, payments are made in bills of exchange on London, and sometimes in the acceptances of the purchasers made payable there, at dates from two to three months. These bills form the great circulating medium of Liverpool, that they are paid and received

---

[72] Parl. Papers, Evidence of Merchants, 1808, p. 48.
[73] Parl. Papers, Report on State of Commercial Credit, 1811 (52), p. 3.
[74] Parl. Papers, Report on Cash Payments, 1819, III (282), p. 179.

by buyers and sellers, and where the date of the bill is more or less than the term of agreement, the difference of interest is added or deducted; . . ."[75]

METHODS OF PAYMENT

The final settlement for goods purchased for Americans or sold to Americans was made in several different ways. Three stand out as particularly prominent: payments might be made (a) by shipments of produce; (b) by drafts drawn on one of the large commercial houses against consignments of cotton or other produce to Great Britain; or (c) by drafts drawn on one of the large Anglo-American banking houses of London on funds secured by shipments of produce to the Continent.[76]

It is evident that in the final analysis all, or the major portion, of the exports from Great Britain must have been paid for by the shipment of produce from the United States, either to Great Britain or to countries with which both the United States and Great Britain had commercial dealings. While this is true for exports as a whole, it does not hold true for particular exports and for particular exporters, for there was no necessary connection between the importer of goods and the exporter of goods.

However, in many cases, such a connection existed; a number of commercial houses stated that they were paid for the goods which they exported from Great Britain by the consignments of produce from America. Bainbridge, a merchant in the American trade, said that he received payment for his shipments to America partly in produce shipped to him on consignment, partly in bills remitted from America, and partly in the proceeds of produce shipped to the Continent.[77] Wiggin, a general exporter to America, also spoke of receiving produce to a certain extent, but said that was a limited part of his business.[78] Withington, a

---

[75] Parl. Papers, Report on Cash Payments, 1819, III (282), p. 105.

[76] Another method which was used, but which does not seem to have been characteristic, was mentioned by one exporter. He stated that certain Manchester houses had drawn drafts on the American purchasers, payable in London six to nine months after date, and accepted by the American purchaser. But he also stated that the exporters of goods from Manchester generally received drafts on merchants of London. Parl. Papers, Evidence of Merchants, 1808, pp. 5-7.

[77] Parl. Papers, Evidence of Merchants, 1808, p. 121.

[78] *Ibid.*, p. 324.

buyer of Manchester goods, received a considerable portion of the sums owed him in the form of American produce.[79] This was true also of Mann, and others in the American trade.[80]

A number of merchants, however, asserted that the principal method of making payment was by bills of exchange. Phillips, for example, said that his house sometimes received produce, but payments were made principally by bills of exchange;[81] Palmer, of the house of John Guest and Company, claimed that produce was rarely received in payment of goods exported.[82]

These bills were drawn upon mercantile houses to which shipments of produce had been made, and were usually at sixty days sight. It was customary for the American merchant or importer to make payments to the agent of the British exporter in America as funds became available. With these funds the British agent purchased bills of exchange, drawn on a London or Liverpool merchant; it was quite rare for the draft remitted to England to be drawn by the person to whom the goods had been sent.[83]

The operations of the firm of Mackensie, Glennie and Company give an excellent illustration of the way in which the payments due British merchants might be effected through consign-

---

[79] Parl. Papers, Evidence of Merchants, 1808, p. 289.

[80] *Ibid.*, p. 57.

[81] *Ibid.*, pp. 9, 16.

[82] *Ibid.*, p. 22.

[83] *Ibid.*, p. 9.

"How does it [the Liverpool firm] receive payment for goods so exported to America? Principally in Bills of Exchange upon England, drawn upon mercantile houses in England; sometimes in produce, but principally in Bills of Exchange."

Ibid., p. 13.

"What is the mode of payment? By notes or by cash to an agent in America, which agent purchases bills with those notes and cash.

"You mean that the agent in America collects the debts due to the houses, and receives the money in American bank notes, or in specie, and buys bills with that property? Not bank notes, notes that are negotiable, that are issued there.

"At what dates are those bills purchased? They are chiefly sixty days; that is the usual date.

.   .   .   .   .

"Then bills remitted from America are not the drafts of the persons to whom the goods are sent from England? Very rarely.

"Of what nature are the drafts and bills remitted from America to England, are they drafts of bankers in America? No; invariably the drafts of merchants."

ments of American produce to the Continent. This firm was established about 1750, and apparently the earlier operations were mainly exporting and importing, but there was a gradual development along the line of international banking, until in the first decade of the nineteenth century we find that the commercial features had dwindled in importance, and the banking business had been enormously expanded. Mr. Glennie, one of the partners, said in 1808 that only about ten per cent of the business of the firm consisted in receiving consignments from America—the other ninety per cent was in receiving remittances from the Continent in payment of American produce shipped there.[84] The extent of the business was very considerable; the managing clerk of the firm estimated that before 1808 it amounted to between one and two million pounds sterling annually.

The funds thus acquired were drawn against by the American exporter, and the bills drawn were usually in favor of manufacturers in Yorkshire, or the exporters of manufactured goods in London.

"We paid away the money in different ways; first by the Americans drawing upon us in America, and selling their bills to the agents of British manufacturers in America; secondly, we used to pay a great many of the manufacturers in this country by orders from our various correspondents in America; as for instance, we receive orders—You will receive remittances from A B C; when you receive them, you will pay Mr. Wallis of Birmingham and . . . such a sum of money."[85]

The firm of Martin, Hope, and Thornely was engaged to some extent in the same line, and the testimony of Mr. Thornely tends to show the importance of this type of business.

"Did you ever receive proceeds of American sales on the Continent of Europe to invest in British produce, and remit to America? Certainly.
"Does that form a large line of trade in this country? It does, but more with London, than with Liverpool."[86]

[84] It was the custom for American ships bound with consignments for the Continent to touch at Falmouth to get orders from such firms as Mackensie, Glennie and Company for landing the goods at the most favorable market. Parl. Papers, Evidence of Merchants, 1808, p. 27 (Evidence of Mr. Glennie); Parl. Papers, Report on Orders in Council, 1812, p. 537.

[85] Parl. Papers, Report on Orders in Council, 1812, p. 464. General authority for statements relating to this firm, ibid., p. 463; and Parl. Papers, Evidence of Merchants, 1808, p. 23.

[86] Parl. Papers, Report on Orders in Council, 1812, p. 350.

A more definite estimate of the extent to which consignments to Europe provided funds for the payment of British manufactured goods was given by Bainbridge:

"Do you think that one-half of the remittances from America is in consignments to the Continent? No, I should think not one-half; I should think about one-third."[87]

It may or may not have been true that one-third of the bills drawn in America, and remitted to Great Britain in the purchase of goods, were in consequence of shipments to the countries of continental Europe; but it appears to be unquestionably true that this formed an important part of the Anglo-American foreign exchange relations.

The American merchant bore a good reputation for prompt payments. Stevenson, a potter dealing directly with America, stated in 1812 that the Americans paid more promptly than any other foreign customer, and in fact, better than the home trade. He found a growing disposition on the part of the Americans to pay cash for their goods.[88] A Birmingham banker testified in the same year to the regularity of payments.

"Have the payments been good? Exceedingly regular and good.
"Have they been improving in regularity? They have always been regular since I knew them.
"Have they increased in promptness? Certainly they have increased in promptness since I knew them.
"Is there any part of the world in which the returns are made more promptly than from America? None more regularly, certainly."[89]

[87] Parl. Papers, Evidence of Merchants, 1808, p. 121.
[88] Parl. Papers, Report on Orders in Council, 1812, p. 162.
[89] *Ibid.,* p. 54.

CHAPTER VI

THE TRADE IN BRITISH MANUFACTURES, 1815-1830

BRITISH TRADE ORGANISATION

DURING the period from 1815 to 1830 we find radical changes and developments in the organisation for the handling of manufactured goods both in Great Britain and in the United States. It was a period when, apparently, the flow of goods from England to America became so voluminous that the older distributive system could no longer cope with it. The manufacturer felt, in the lowered unit cost resulting from a greater volume of products, a constant pressure to increase his production, and found that he could no longer rely on the British merchant to purchase his entire output. It was, therefore, necessary for him to become an active merchandising agent. On the other hand, the merchant did not feel it profitable for him to purchase goods in Great Britain to sell in a foreign market when he might have to face the competition of the manufacturer himself, disposing of his surplus stocks. Hence we find the manufacturer necessarily assuming a larger proportion of the risks of marketing, and the merchant to a greater degree than formerly acting as a commission agent for the manufacturer.

This situation, resulting from the far-reaching changes in the technique of production, was complicated by conditions in America. There was not only an extraordinary demand for goods evidenced at the close of the War of 1812, and consequent on the more or less complete cessation of the Anglo-American trade for a number of years, but a real increase in the demand for these goods, due to the growing numbers and purchasing power of the American people. So we have not only a case of goods produced under conditions of diminishing cost, but, for most of the goods, we find a very elastic demand. In other words, the conditions were very favorable for a rapid and speculative development of the foreign trade between Great Britain and America.

THE CONSIGNMENT SYSTEM OF GREAT BRITAIN

We have seen that in many lines it was customary to consign goods for sale in a foreign market to a commission merchant; the American cotton planters or merchants consigned cotton to Liverpool to be sold on commission, and British merchants consigned manufactures to the United States and to other markets for sale there for what they would bring. In a number of instances British manufacturers consigned their own goods to foreign houses before 1815, but we have shown that it was not the customary mode of procedure. When textiles or hardware were consigned to the American market the risk of sale was, in the majority of cases, on the British exporting merchant, and not on the manufacturer. In this period, however, the manfacturer assumed to a much greater extent the risks of marketing as well as of manufacturing.

Although the nature of the system of consignments has been discussed previously, it may be well to state that by this system we mean that the manufacturer made up his goods to stock, and not on the basis of definite orders. Those orders given him by merchants of Great Britain, or by foreign merchants, were, of course, filled, and the surplus stock was then shipped either to an agent of the manufacturer placed in America—or in some other foreign country—or was shipped to a merchant in Great Britain, who consigned it to a similar agent in America. In either case the risks of loss were assumed by the manufacturer.

Consignments by the Manufacturer to His Agent in America. As soon as it was practicable after peace had been restored between Great Britain and the United States, goods which had been in storage in Great Britain during the war were rushed to America for sale; the success which attended these first ventures encouraged the manufacturers to prepare more goods for the American market, and in order to hasten the sale of these goods they established agents of their own in America in many cases. An American writer described in 1820 the beginning of this type of business:

"They [the large manufacturers of England] sent forth a swarm of agents, accompanied with a flood of their fabrics. This inundated our market, and at the close of the year 1816, the United States were overwhelmed with an excess of foreign commodities, partly on account of our own citizens, and partly on account of foreign speculators."[90]

[90] *Trade and Commerce of New York*, 1820, p. 22.

Mention of the British agents in America was made by the woolen manufacturers who in 1826 complained of the system of consignment to agents.

"The English manufacturers have exported their goods to their agents in this country, for sale, and for more than a year past, they have been and now are continually disposing of them in large quantities at public vendue, at little or no profit, and often at a great sacrifice."[91]

That the woolen manufacturers anticipated that such competition would be the ruin of the domestic manufactures is indicated in the following quotation:

"Since that period [1821] our markets have been overstocked with British woolen goods, which have been sold on account of the manufacturer or British merchant at auction and at prices less than their actual cost, the continuance of which even for a short time must mean the ruin and destruction of the woolen manufactures of this country."[92]

In a letter appearing in the *Liverpool Mercury* in 1832—and apparently written by an American—we find a complaint against the system of consignments by the manufacturers. The writer noted the overstocking of the American market with British manufactured goods consigned by the manufacturers: and apparently he considered the situation rather critical, for he said:

"One thing must be done—the merchants of the United States must cease purchasing or the manufacturers cease from consigning. If the latter were the case the merchant would be able to buy a needful supply, and the market kept more regular. . . ."[93]

Still later evidence of consignments by manufacturers to agents was afforded in the testimony of a Glasgow witness before the Parliamentary Committee in 1834. He stated that before 1816 the manufacturer was accustomed to sell to the merchant, but that since that date and especially since the year 1826 "it has been the custom for the manufacturer to consign his goods to an agent abroad; . . ."[94]

[91] Niles, *Register*, 1826, vol. 31, p. 185.
[92] Shaw, *Wool Trade of the United States*, 1909, p. 27. This is apparently a quotation or a paraphrase from a Memorial of citizens of Albany in 1824.
[93] *Liverpool Mercury*, March 2, 1832, p. 72.
[94] Parl. Papers, Report on Hand-Loom Weavers, 1834, p. 100.

A witness in 1833 testified that some of the cotton manufacturers shipped their own goods abroad almost exclusively. When asked if it were reckoned good policy to do so, he replied that there was "a difference of opinion."[95] Davidson, a Glasgow manufacturer, said that "it is now very generally the case that goods are shipped by the manufacturer; the shipments by merchants having establishments of their own abroad, are, I should think, . . . very limited, . . ."[96] Finlay in 1833 ascribed the low rate of profits in the cotton trade to the "practice which has prevailed of late years, of the manufacturer making large consignments of his productions to foreign countries. . . ."[97] Joshua Bates' testimony on the subject of consignments was as follows:

"Do you know whether the manufacturers of this country are not in the habit of sending their goods to foreign markets, where they are placed in depot, and held for the demand as it occurs there; and where they employ an agent to effect a sale for them? Yes, they do."[98]

Another witness, who testified in 1834, gave the following as his version of the system of consignments by the manufacturer, and its causes:

"I think that the very great fall consequent upon everything from war to peace annihilated many of the foreign merchants, and they have not been able to buy themselves as they did before, and as a natural consequence manufacturers will frequently, at the solicitation of the foreign merchant, send goods out on his own account."[99]

A merchant of Glasgow spoke of the "injudicious mode by which foreign markets are supplied to a great extent by the manufacturers of Glasgow of late years; that is, by consignments on the part of the manufacturers of these goods themselves, . . ."[100] Still another witness stated that there was in 1834 little buying of goods in Glasgow by merchants for export. Practically all the business was on consignment.[101]

Consignments by Manufacturers to Commission Merchants in Great Britain. It is clear that many manufacturers shipped their surplus output directly to their own agents resident abroad,

[95] Parl. Papers, Report on Manufactures, 1833, p. 299.
[96] Parl. Papers, Report on Hand-Loom Weavers, 1834, p. 137.
[97] Parl. Papers, Report on Manufactures, 1833, p. 35.
[98] *Ibid.*, p. 61.
[99] Parl. Papers, Report on Hand-Loom Weavers, 1834, p. 120.
[100] *Ibid.*, p. 163.
[101] *Ibid.*, p. 108.

but, as has been said, this was not the only method in use; the manufacturer might consign his goods to a merchant in his home city, or in one of the port cities, and it is but natural to expect to find him doing this. The merchant had established trade relations with American correspondents which could not be immediately duplicated by the manufacturer; he had the specialised knowledge of the needs of the different markets, and of the technique of shipping, which could be of value to the manufacturer. Therefore, if circumstances were such as to discourage him from purchasing directly from the manufacturer, he could at least serve him by acting as his commission agent.

We find this method of disposing of goods quite common throughout the period. The manufacturer consigned his goods to the merchant, who reconsigned them to his agent or correspondent in America, and settled with the manufacturer when he received the proceeds of their sale in America. Consignment to commission merchants became so common a method of exporting goods that a witness declared in 1834 that there were not more than three exporting merchants in Liverpool:

". . . from the best information there are not now more than three exporting merchants at Liverpool. The manufacturer consigns his goods to a commission house, which again consigns them to some person abroad, and he draws upon the shipper."[102]

Consignments to commission merchants offered an advantage to the manufacturer over the system of consignment directly to an agent in America, because the British commission merchants were usually willing to make advances to the amount of two-thirds or three-fourths of the value of the goods so consigned. It will be noted that in the above quotation mention is made of the custom of drawing a bill on the commission merchant; this was generally the way in which the advances were made.

The custom of drawing bills of exchange against consignments became almost the rule. Most of the Manchester goods were consigned and drawn against.[103] In fact, so general did this custom become that some manufacturers who did not need the advances themselves, but who were not in a position to sell the goods through their own foreign agent, and consequently had to make

[102] Parl. Papers, Report on Hand-Loom Weavers, 1834, p. 424.
[103] Parl. Papers, Report on Commercial Distress, 1847-1848, vol. XXIV (31), p. 187.

use of the commission merchants, were said to have been forced to accept the advances, because otherwise the merchant would see to it that the goods on which he had made advances were sold first.[104]

Mackensie, a Scottish manufacturer, testified to the ease with which a manufacturer could get advances, amounting to a large proportion of the value of his goods:

"The system of trade at the present moment is changed considerably to what it was twenty or thirty years ago; the manufacturer who cannot go direct or send his own agent to see the goods sold upon the spot, consigns them to a broker or agent, with certain powers to sell, and he (the broker) advances a certain sum of money; . . . There is a very curious system now carried on at Glasgow; money is so very plentiful; if a man can produce £500 worth of goods, he will get £400 advance upon them from some of the monied men of the city."[105]

This practice tended to encourage speculation and reckless manufacturing. It was possible for a manufacturer to maintain himself in business for a considerable time by means of these advances, and some of them consigned simply in order to receive the advances. A witness was asked in 1847 if it had not been the practice of manufacturers to send out their goods, "not in consequence of Orders, but upon Speculation, for the purpose of getting Advances upon the goods so sent out," and replied that they had done so—"largely so, to all Quarters."[106] Another witness, a general merchant of London, Liverpool, and Glasgow, asserted that the prevalence of the system of advances on consignments was the chief source of the unhealthy state of the cotton trade.

"Then you consider that the only circumstances which affects the cotton trade, and renders one branch of it unhealthy, is the speculation which is entered upon by the manufacturers in sending their goods, upon consignment, to very distant markets, . . .?"

"I think that one circumstance, which is omitted in the question, is the principal cause of the unhealthy character of the trade to which I allude; namely, the advances that are made upon goods before sending them."[107]

[104] Parl. Papers, Report on Hand-Loom Weavers, 1834, p. 108.
[105] *Ibid.*, p. 51.
[106] Parl. Papers, Report on Commercial Distress, 1847-1848, vol. XXIV (31), p. 234.
[107] Parl. Papers, Report on Manufactures, 1833, p. 36.

Some of the commission houses and firms of questionable repute dealt in a similar way with the smaller manufacturers. But they were not content with accepting consignments, and making advances—they actively sought them:

"Immediately after the peace of the country was consolidated, there were men issued out from Liverpool, calling themselves merchants, going around from warehouse to warehouse, like number carriers, like hawkers of goods, and requesting consignments; they said they were doing business with Rio Janeiro, and other ports and they could as well sell £10,000 of goods along with theirs as not."[108]

These houses were given the opprobrious name of "slaughterhouses," because of the effect which their operations had on the smaller manufacturers and on the trade in general. It was asserted that they had been the cause of the ruin of hundreds of manufacturers by selling goods at a sacrifice to meet the bills drawn upon them by the manufacturer.

"Suppose a manufacturer in this neighborhood is manufacturing to the extent of 500£ a week, and a commission man the same. The London salesman, in consigning your goods to him, allows you to draw 450£ against him as a bill, to assist you in going on with the business. At the expiration of the three months' time, when the bill becomes due, perhaps he has not disposed of the goods that he has got in hand, and at such times he is forced into the market with those goods, because he will not lose his credit as the acceptor of that bill: he throws the goods into the market at a percentage lower to meet his engagements coming due. Thousands and thousands have been doing that way, and are to the present day. Another manufacturer selling legitimately through the market, is compelled to compete against the prices of those men."[109]

But the manufacturer might be victimised by the commission merchant to whom he consigned his goods in various other ways. One report cited evidence showing that a certain house which had thus solicited consignments on the ground that it could handle goods in addition to its own, had never exported any of its own goods, and had reconsigned the textiles consigned to it to commissioners in South America, where they were sold at a price which ruined twelve manufacturing firms.[110] Again there

108 Parl. Papers, Report on Hand-Loom Weavers, 1834, p. 424.
109 Parl. Papers, Report on Condition of Frame Work Knitters, 1845, vol. XXIV, p. 324.
110 Parl. Papers, Report on Hand-Loom Weavers, 1834, p. 424.

was the possibility of downright dishonesty in dealing with the manufacturers.

"There are many men in London who get goods consigned to them from the manufacturer; they begin with a trifle, they are encouraged to increase their manufactures; they draw upon them to a half or two-thirds of the value; they afterwards pretend that they have not or cannot sell the goods; the advances are demanded, and the sales made by number one, and number two pockets the difference and they take the rest of the goods to meet the balance; these should be called slaughter-houses; but that applied to London, and not to Preston and Manchester, where men sell for what they can get."[111]

It was asserted that at that time (1834) there were fewer of these "slaughter-houses" in London than there had been twenty years earlier, but that the number at the seaports had increased.[112]

The method of disposing of manufactured goods by consignments by the manufacturer was not confined to the American trade, although that trade offered an excellent field for its development, but was characteristic of trade to other parts of the world as well. The following evidence, given by an agent interested in the trade to India, shows its prevalence in the export of goods to the Far East:

"Are you aware that a considerable portion of the manufactured goods sent to India, are sent by other houses, on account of the manufacturers?

"The manufacturers, in some instances, I understand, send out goods upon their own account, the agents or merchants in London making them advances of one-half or two-thirds of the invoice amount, and settling with them for the remainder when they get the returns from India."[113]

Again, advances were not made by the British merchants alone. In some instances consignments were made to the London branch house of a foreign concern, or to his British agent, if he did not maintain a separate establishment in Great Britain. The branch house, or agent, allowed the manufacturer to draw upon it for the amount of the advance, and accepted the bill when

[111] Parl. Papers, Reports on Hand-Loom Weavers, 1834, p. 348.
[112] *Ibid.*, p. 423.
[113] Parl. Papers, Report on Manufactures, 1833, p. 189.

drawn.[114] Davidson indicated the reliance placed by some manufacturers on such foreign houses when he said:

"I never made a shipment to a foreign market that was not recommended and sanctioned by an agent here, either himself a member of the firm abroad to whom they were consigned, or acting for them in the capacity of an agent."[115]

In some cases the advances were in the form of cash, but this was not the general usage. Usually the advances took the form of bills of exchange drawn by the manufacturer on the merchant, and accepted by him. These bills could then be discounted in the general bill market, and the manufacturer placed in possession of ready cash. Sometimes the bills were of short date, but more often they ran for several months. In the India trade the bills generally ran for six, nine, or even twelve months, and were frequently renewed, if the sale of the goods had not been effected by the time the bill matured.[116]

The manufacturer making consignments assumed all the costs of shipping. The rates of commission to different markets varied, but it was estimated that the shipping expenses and commissions, including "del credere," amounted to about ten per cent of the value of the goods.[117]

MERCHANTS EXPORTING ON THEIR OWN ACCOUNT

While the system of consignments seems to have been of major importance throughout this period, the fact should not be lost sight of that there were other methods in vogue at the same time. The exporting merchant of Great Britain did not cease to purchase goods on his own account, when he felt that he could do so advantageously, nor did the American altogether stop buying. Probably towards the end of the period the purchases of both the British merchant and the American merchant became more voluminous.

We have evidence of the activity of some of the merchants in purchasing the output of the small manufacturers. It was asserted that there were in Manchester many large purchasing houses specialising in buying up at favorable prices the goods

114 Parl. Papers, Report on Hand-Loom Weavers, 1834, p. 105.
115 *Ibid.*, p. 163.
116 *Ibid.*, 1834, p. 108.
117 *Ibid.*, 1834, p. 108.

made by the small manufacturer; they did not advance on consignment, but bought outright.

"There are large purchasing houses in Manchester. There are in the country in various places small manufacturers. These classes, having plenty of money, are always ready to purchase under favorable circumstances such productions as the smaller manufacturers fabricate; they do not lend them money by consignment upon them, they buy them as cheaply as they can; and so far as it is cheaper, from their necessities, than they are able to produce them, it has a tendency to reduce the price of labor."[118]

The goods thus obtained were consigned for sale to the foreign agents or correspondents of the merchants, or were used to fill orders sent them by American merchants. In many cases, however, purchases were made by the merchants only as the American orders came in to them. There seems to have been a considerable volume of purchases made by the commission houses, acting as agents for the American, around the year 1830.[119] When a merchant received an order for goods from America, he purchased them from the manufacturer for cash in some cases, but usually he settled for them by means of a trade acceptance at three or four months sight. Frequently he would then consign the goods to a commission merchant at Liverpool, say, and draw on him for three-fourths of their value. John Ewart, of the firm of Ewart, Meyers and Company, of Liverpool and London, an importing and exporting firm doing a large volume of business with America, testified on this point:

"Supposing that a merchant resident at Birmingham can purchase 10,000£ of goods for his acceptances at four months, may he not send those goods to Liverpool, and draw for 6,000£ or 7,000£ upon them at four months' date?

"I believe that he might; I know that a merchant in Liverpool, having a house abroad to which such goods are to go, having full possession and control of the sale of them will give an accommodation to the owner."[120]

[118] Parl. Papers, Report on Hand-Loom Weavers, 1834, p. 348.
[119] Parl. Papers, Report on Manufactures, 1833, p. 253. The British commission merchant charged a commission of two and one-half per cent for executing orders for the American merchant.
Liverpool Mercury, March 2, 1832, p. 72.
[120] Parl. Papers, Report on Manufactures, 1833, p. 252.

John Slack protested against this method of carrying on business and professed to find in this system of buying by means of acceptances, and then receiving advances from another merchant, the source of much possible danger and embarrassment to the mercantile community:

"I have, in a former publication, given my opinion of the ruinous consequences of buying goods for acceptances, which is now too much the prevailing practice; for when such is the case, and any house becomes so engaged and has to contend with a dull and declining market for a month or six weeks, sales cannot be made but at a loss, and a number of acceptances being out, which must or ought to be provided for, a sacrifice of property will necessarily be unavoidable. Sometimes goods are placed in the hands of an agent or commission salesman, who is probably asked to advance £300 or £350 upon a nominal value of £500; when, if he gives anything, it will be his own promissory note, or he must be drawn upon by this necessitous house, to meet some acceptance just upon their becoming due."[121]

This practice of purchasing goods for acceptances and then seeking advances from some merchant or agent was said to have existed to a greater degree before 1830 than later, when it was said to have been "of no considerable extent."[122] Thomas Wiggin, a banker, testified that he had known of the practice, but believed that it was not particularly prevalent in 1833.

"Have you known the kind of business referred to of goods purchased for acceptances, and sent to Liverpool, and the party immediately drawing for three-fourths of the amount?
"I have heard of such transactions in former years, but within the last two or three years my own correspondents have paid cash almost uniformly for their goods without their aid."[123]

CREDIT

Credit Terms. The shortening of the term of credit given by the manufacturer to the merchant is a very noticeable feature of this period. We have seen that during the years before 1815 the time of payment was usually quite extended, but the profits which were gained in foreign trade after 1815 were apparently so extensive as to enable the merchants to take advantage of the lower prices which a shorter credit made possible.

[121] Slack, *Commercial Caution*, 1835, p. 19.
[122] Parl. Papers, Report on Manufactures, 1833, p. 123.
[123] *Ibid.*, p. 122.

The woolens of Leeds and Huddersfield were sold around 1815 at six and eight months' credit; but by 1828 the credit had been shortened to a month or two, and a great deal of the cloth was sold for cash.[124] John Brooke, a woolen merchant, averred that the credit period on Yorkshire cloth had decreased, and stated that it was customary to sell for cash or short credit.[125] A yarn manufacturer claimed that the credit in his trade was a bill at two months at the end of four months, as contrasted with the nine months formerly allowed, and said that the buyers paid cash more often than they used to.[126]

The cotton trade shows an even shorter period of credit than we found in the woolen trade. Smith, a commission merchant for the sale of cotton goods and yarn, in Manchester, stated the custom of the trade to be payment for the goods one month after sale by a bill of three months. Any merchant who wished to pay cash was given a discount of one and one-half per cent, and Smith claimed that "nearly all the payments are made in cash in our trade." Smith noted further that the credit had shortened generally; that there were many goods sold on one day which were paid for on the following day.[127]

The term of credit given to purchasers of silks was stated by Shaw, a commission merchant, to be five months, with a two and one-half per cent discount for cash. In former years silk had been sold on ten months' credit, with a five per cent discount for cash. Two-thirds of the purchasers in 1833 paid cash and took the discount.[128]

Hardware was sold to the domestic trade, according to statements made in 1833, at six months' credit, but frequently the merchants paid cash on delivery. Some of the Americans purchased by acceptances at two or three months after the delivery of the goods at Liverpool; others, by acceptances of four months after the date of the invoice. In response to the inquiry of the committee as to whether there had been any change in the credit

[124] Parl. Papers, Report on British Wool Trade, 1828, p. 136. It was stated in 1823 that certain Blackwell-Hall factors sold woolens for export at *twelve months' credit*. Parl. Papers, Report on Merchants, 1823, p. 207.

[125] Parl. Papers, Report on Manufactures, 1833, p. 118.

[126] *Ibid.*, p. 161.

[127] *Ibid.*, p. 560. *Cf.* also, Report on Bank of England Charter, 1831-1832, p. 339.

[128] Parl. Papers, Report on Manufactures, 1833, p. 91.

terms during the past ten or fifteen years, the witness said that he believed that the American trade in hardware had usually been conducted on those terms.[129]

The shortening of the credit period seems to have become a permanent feature of the foreign and domestic trade of Great Britain. Payments for goods in cash were more prominent in 1833 than before or after that date. One merchant even said that he thought "it has become almost a system to pay money in Liverpool and London."[130] We cannot, however, accept that statement as applying generally to any of the periods under discussion, for the sale of goods on credit prevailed throughout the first half of the nineteenth century.

Banks and Discount Houses. The relation of the banks and the note brokers to the foreign trade organisation of this period is of real significance. We have spoken of the advances made by the commission merchants to the manufacturers as if such advances depended entirely on the capital of the merchants. Doubtless this was true to a certain extent; certainly they must have been possessed of considerable amounts of capital to engage in the business at all. Yet they in turn were dependent on the banks. A report on mercantile customs in 1823 noted that the merchants to whom goods were consigned were accustomed to apply to the banks to support them in the carrying of this credit.

". . . and it is proved to the entire satisfaction of your Committee, not only that the merchants of Great Britain are constantly in the habit of making advances on merchandise consigned to them for sale, to the extent of two-thirds or three-quarters of their value, but that they are also in the habit of obtaining advances themselves from bankers, corn factors, brokers and others upon goods so consigned to them, as well as upon their own merchandise; this appears to have resulted necessarily from the great increase in our foreign trade, and it is stated by the most respectable witnesses to be practiced to such an extent by all classes of merchants (not excepting houses of the highest respectability) that it may be considered essential to the carrying on of trade that it be continued."[131]

This quotation is rather general in nature, and applied both to the import and the export trade. The following quotation has

129 Parl. Papers, Report on Manufactures, 1833, p. 187.
130 *Ibid.*, p. 64.
131 Parl. Papers, Report on Merchants, 1823, p. 11.

specific reference to the consignments of manufactures, and shows rather clearly the dependence of the merchants making advances upon the other capitalists:

"In times of distress, when no ready market presents itself, the manufacturers are still obliged to purchase materials, in order to prevent the frightful distress which would otherwise be experienced by their workmen, and they must of course continue to pay wages. In this situation . . . they of course avail themselves of the assistance of their factors to the extent of the means of the latter; but as these gentlemen stand in the same relation to several manufacturers, it becomes absolutely necessary that they should be enabled to obtain advances upon manufactured goods; so that they may continue to extend assistance to their principals; and there have been times, not very remote, when it is probable that such goods had become a security to capitalists to the extent of one-half the entire stock of manufactured goods.[132]

The frequency with which the merchants and manufacturers in the evidence quoted above, have spoken of purchases by acceptances must have been noted. The term *acceptances* meant of course bills of exchange drawn upon some merchant and accepted by him. The whole purpose in drawing such bills of exchange was to put the manufacturer in the possession of immediate funds, of ready cash. To obtain these funds, a large discount market was necessary. This discount market was supplied by the banks and the note and bill brokers who were willing to discount the bills of exchange for the holders. That it was very extensive seems clear from the fact that except in times of panic (as in 1836, when the Bank of England refused to rediscount some of the bills accepted by the large Anglo-American houses) there is no evidence of any difficulty experienced by a manufacturer or merchant in getting his acceptances converted into cash. If any one of these discount houses wished, it could provide itself with funds by rediscounting at the Bank of England, either at the main office in London, or at one of the branches—at Liverpool, for example.

It seems to me that the importance of the banking and credit facilities open to the British merchant and manufacturer, and through them to the American merchant, and even to the American consumer, cannot be overestimated. This factor alone would be sufficient to explain why the United States naturally turned

[132] Parl. Papers, Report on Merchants, 1823, p. 12.

to Great Britain for her manufactured goods; no other nation in Europe could supply America with goods on such convenient terms of payment.

THE AUCTION SYSTEM IN AMERICA

The discussion thus far has centered largely around the operations of the manufacturer and the merchant in Great Britain. Quite as interesting and as important is the situation which developed in the United States in the period after the War of 1812, when the manufactured goods of Great Britain were flowing into the country in such unprecedented quantities.

It has been shown that in the years before 1812, the greater part of the goods imported into the United States from Great Britain was on the account of, and at the risk of the British merchant, but that, at the same time, the American importer, either himself purchasing in England or sending his orders to manufacturers or merchants, was by no means an unimportant figure. The goods which he thus had shipped to the United States were generally sold to a more or less regular circle of customers, and at private sale. Each importing merchant, whether importing on his own account or acting as a consignee, had his own clientele, consisting of jobbers, who made up assortments for the country stores, of large city retailers, and, in some cases, of large country dealers.[133] Business was conducted along fairly conservative lines, and the volume of business was regulated by the known or estimated demands of the clients of the importer.

In contrast to this method of carrying on the import trade we find, after 1815, more and more of the speculative element in business. In a Memorial submitted to Congress in 1819 the complaint was made that the conservative merchant had been supplanted by the foreign speculator.

"Our commerce was, at first, carried on by resident merchants, whose prudence and experience restrained importations within due bounds; . . . But for some years past, and especially since the universal peace in Europe, and the conclusion of the late war, those regular traders have found themselves supplanted by foreign merchants and manufacturers, or desperate speculators. . . ."[134]

---

[133] *Facts*, 1831, p. 6. It was stated that nine-tenths of the purchases were made at private sale.

[134] *Memorial . . . of New York*, 1819 (9), p. 6.

We have already noted this speculative element in Great Britain as it affected the merchants and manufacturers. It was evidenced in the development of the consignment business, in the assumption by the manufacturer of marketing risks. In the United States the increase in consignments, and the swelling in the volume of goods to be sold, resulted in the Auction System. It is with the development of the auction system that we shall be concerned in this section.[135]

THE DEVELOPMENT OF THE AUCTION SYSTEM

The auction was not unknown in the United States before 1812, but as a method of disposing of goods it was not in the best repute. Goods which had been damaged, second-hand goods, and goods for which immediate cash was required, were placed in the hands of an auctioneer for sale. During the War of 1812, however, it came to be more generally used. The prizes captured by the armed merchantmen were often sold at auction, and such consignments of foreign goods as were smuggled in, or brought in by circuitous routes, were sold in this way, as the quickest and most convenient method of disposing of them. Thus by the time trade was reopened with Great Britain, the business world had become accustomed to this method of disposing of goods.[136]

During the war great quantities of manufactures had been concentrated in *dépôts* at various places in Canada, at Halifax, and Bermuda, while the warehouses of Liverpool were crammed with packages and bales, some of them ordered by American merchants, some of them bought on speculation by merchants, and others the property of manufacturers, but all of them intended for shipment the moment trade relations could be resumed.[137] Evidence of the extent of these accumulations in Liverpool is afforded in the evidence taken before the Parliamentary Committee in 1812. For example, Mr. Rathbone, a shipping merchant, had about two thousand packages, valued at £200,000, in his warehouses ready for shipment.[138] Mr. Brown, a Liverpool merchant, stated that he had in storage "about six hundred pack-

---

[135] For a more exhaustive treatment of the auction system along certain lines, the reader is referred to Westerfield, *Early History of American Auctions,* in the Trans. of the Conn. Acad., May, 1920, pp. 159-210.

[136] *Facts,* 1831, p. 7. Hunt, *Merchants' Magazine,* 1844, vol. X, p. 156. *Trade and Commerce of New York,* 1820, p. 24.

[137] Hunt, *Merchants' Magazine,* 1844, vol. X, p. 156.

[138] Parl. Papers, Report on Orders in Council, 1812, p. 429.

ages of hardware, calicoes, muslins, and a variety of other articles . . . difficult now to enumerate, destined for Baltimore, and some for Philadelphia,'' which were worth about £100,000.[139]

Immediately upon the conclusion of peace, and the reopening of trade channels, these goods were sent to the United States, and American importing merchants dispatched orders for large quantities of goods. The demand for them was very eager, for the supply was very low, especially in New York. The auction offered the most convenient medium of sale, and was used quite generally.[140] The success which attended these first ventures en-

[139] Parl. Papers, Report on Orders in Council, 1812, p. 294.

[140] The method of sale by auction is well described in the *Memorial of the Auctioneers* of 1821.

''Sales of dry goods are made at auction by the package or by the piece, and this is the only distinction to be observed in all the variety of the trade. Package sales being much more important in amount and more attractive by the assortments of merchandise they combine, excite most interest and are attended with greatest competition. When the sale is of magnitude, it is generally advertised in the principal commercial cities with an enumeration of the articles to be sold. Printed catalogues are prepared, specifying the term of credit, with the other conditions of sale, and detailing the contents of each package, the number of pieces, the varieties of quality, by number or otherwise, and the lengths, all of which are guaranteed to the purchasers. . . .

''The packages are arranged in lots, corresponding with their number on the catalogue, and are exhibited, sometimes two or three days before the sale, sometimes but one; the length of the exhibition regulated by the magnitude of the sale. When the goods are prepared for inspection, the purchasers are invited, by a public notice in the papers, to examine them. Where it is necessary for an advantageous examination, whole packages are opened and displayed: where it can be made with more convenience from samples, one or more pieces of each quality is exhibited; and where there are many packages exactly corresponding, only one is shown. Pattern cards are exhibited, displaying the assortment of colors, etc. The purchaser receives every information and facility that can contribute to his convenience and protect him from mistakes. The goods are arranged with so much attention to the accommodation of the purchasers, that three or four packages might be examined with care and accuracy in one day.

''Package sales are resorted to when entire cargoes are to be sold, or where the quantity of goods is too great to be disposed of in detail. Large assortments of merchandise are daily offered at piece sales, where packages are opened and the goods sold in small or large lots, as may most tend to the interest of the seller, and the convenience of the purchaser; these sales are regular and systematic, being held by each auctioneer of extensive business on two or more specific days in each week, and are principally depended upon by the retailers, as well as the larger dealers for their uniform supplies.'' *Memorial of Auctioneers of New York*, 1821 (37), pp. 4-6.

couraged the merchants and other speculators to send fresh orders to Great Britain, and so a stimulus was given to the British manufacturer to increase his output.

The period of very brisk foreign trade was, however, short-lived. The huge quantities which were constantly being poured into America soon satisfied the demand of the country. Commencing in 1816, and continuing through 1817 and 1818, the price of these goods fell to such an extent that it was said that many articles could scarcely be sold for more than enough to cover the duties. A setback to the import trade was thus given, which was almost paralysing in its effects.

Contemporary evidence of the distress and confusion obtaining in 1816 is afforded by the following extract from a letter written from New York to the *Liverpool Mercury*:

" 'The people at Leeds must be crazy. They certainly will not get returns for one-half of the amount they have shipped. You can conceive of nothing so appalling as the state of trade here. Among the British goods merchants particularly, bankruptcies are very frequent, enormous in amount, and ruinous in their settlement; and the dry goods (especially low woolens) are selling under the hammer at a loss of thirty to sixty per cent. No private sales can be made, as from 400 to 1200 packages are sold by auction each week. No parallel to the present sufferings of the trade can be found in the history of this country, and it is likely to continue so for your countrymen are determined to send goods here till they are all ruined. . . .' "[141]

The next week the *Mercury* noted that "the Electra from Philadelphia has reached the Downs, laden almost entirely with British manufactures, returned by the persons to whom they were consigned, not being able to meet with a sale, even at twenty and fifty per cent loss on the prime cost."[142] An American writer, in 1831, described the effect which the sudden increase in the volume of imports had on the importing merchant and jobber of America. He said:

"This prostrated *almost* every importer and jobber. I scarce know one of the former who escaped; and those of the latter who weathered the storm were crippled for a long time afterwards."[143]

For a time, therefore, few orders for goods were sent to Eng-

[141] *Liverpool Mercury*, November 22, 1816.
[142] *Ibid.*, November 29, 1816.
[143] *Facts*, 1831, p. 8.

land, and the manufacturers found their stocks mounting rapidly. In the effort to dispose of the surplus production manufacturers shipped more than had been ordered by the American merchants.

"... there are very few respectable importers of British goods in the United States who have not received much greater quantities of them than they directed to be sent out—and vast and valuable cargoes have been, besides, forwarded 'to order' or 'for sale.' "[144]

But this did not fully answer the purpose of the British manufacturers, and many of them found it expedient to send out their own agents to enable them more quickly to sell the surplus. Consignments of goods were made to these agents, who immediately placed the goods in the hands of an auctioneer for sale. The auctioneer frequently signed the bonds at the customs house for the payment of the import duties, and made advances to the agents. As the goods were often sold for cash, it was possible to remit the funds within a very short time to the manufacturer abroad, who was thus enabled to continue manufacturing on a speculative basis.[145]

Thus the auction, which came into prominence through the force of circumstances, remained for many years as a most vital factor in the American marketing organisation, and proved itself a-formidable rival of the more conservative American importer; and the auctioneers became individuals of considerable wealth and authority in the business world. The circumstances surrounding the birth of the auction system were described as follows by an anonymous author in 1820:

"The embarrassments of 1816-17 compelled the holders of merchandise to effect sales. This threw, at one time, into the hands of the auctioneers, almost the whole trade of the city. What accident gave them, they have been able to retain. They now possess the monopoly of a large part of the trade of New York. The foreign merchant and manufacturer, through them, has taken the trade out of our own hands."[146]

EFFECTS OF AUCTIONS ON AMERICAN IMPORTERS

The effect of the system of consignments and sales by auction on the position of the American importing merchant was a fre-

---

[144] Niles, *Register*, 1816, vol. X, p. 322.
[145] *Trade and Commerce of New York*, 1820, p. 25.
[146] *Trade and Commerce of New York*, 1820, p. 25.

quent subject of complaint. The writer quoted above stated that "the manufacturers of Birmingham and Manchester, in England, have become the traders of New York."[147] There is much testimony to show the current belief that auctions were driving the American importer out of business. A Memorial of 1820 asserted that:

"A large amount of American capital, employed by some of the most respectable houses, hitherto engaged in the import trade, has, also, been forced out of it, by the superior advantages and obvious rivalship of those who work on foreign account. . . ."[148]

A writer in Niles' *Register* declared that ". . . many of our most experienced, intelligent, and wealthy merchants, were compelled to do business on a very limited scale; others to cease importing altogether, for the consumption of the country."[149] It was claimed that in Baltimore there was, in 1824, hardly one large dry goods importing house, because of the competition of the foreign consignor, but "a dozen would be established, we are told, were this desolating system restrained as it should be."[150] A writer asserted in 1825 that there could be no doubt that the greater part of the business of importing dry goods, hardware, etc., was controlled by foreigners.[151] In the same year it was estimated that three-fourths of the dry goods imported into New York were imported on foreign account.

"By an investigation of the manifests of cargoes entered at New York, it has been proven, that three-fourths of all the dry goods of cotton, wool, linen, and silk, etc., received in that city were on foreign account, and even a greater proportion of many other valuable articles, though of some additional property only one-half or two-thirds were the property of foreign merchants and manufacturers."[152]

Another estimate was that of 32,000 packages of dry goods imported into New York in 1819 only 8,000 packages were owned by American importers.[153]

In view of the practical unanimity of opinion, we are impelled

---

147 *Trade and Commerce of New York*, 1820, p. 25.
148 *Memorial of the Merchants of Baltimore*, 1820 (30), p. 4.
149 Niles, *Register*, 1825, vol. XXVII, p. 289.
150 *Ibid.*, 1824, vol. XXV, p. 241.
151 *Ibid.*, 1825, vol. XXVII, p. 305.
152 *Ibid.*, 1825, vol. XXVII, p. 289. *Cf.* also p. 273.
153 *Ibid.*, 1820, vol. XVII, p. 416.

to believe that the system of consignments and sale by auction did very seriously interfere with the business of the American importer from Europe. The attention which was paid to the efforts of the American importer after 1830 indicates also that he had not been particularly prominent in the period before 1830. But it is, of course, absurd to conclude that the American importer was entirely eliminated. He was active in other branches of foreign commerce, to a large extent the carrying trade between the United States and Great Britain was in the hands of American shipping merchants, and we may be sure that any favorable opportunity for purchasing goods on his own account was not neglected.

EXPLANATION OF THE RISE OF THE AUCTION SYSTEM

Contemporary writers on this subject advanced many arguments and theories to account for this dwarfing of the importance of the American importer. One which constantly recurred was that fraudulent invoices enabled the consignor to escape a part of the custom duties, and consequently to sell at a lower price. Thus, it was asserted that:

"It is a common custom, and one well understood by merchants, that many foreign importers, resident in this country, (and who do nearly all their business by auction) are in the constant habit of receiving two invoices of each parcel of goods."[154]

One of these invoices was for the purpose of entering the goods; the other contained the actual cost of the goods. More concrete evidence, however, was adduced. It was claimed that one English manufacturer had admitted that he always invoiced the goods at twenty per cent less than cost.[155] Again, it was stated that "we have detected at this port upward of one hundred invoices fraudulently charged at five to one hundred per cent below the value of the goods."[156]

That this unscrupulous undervaluation of imports was practiced seems scarcely open to question; and in so far as it was resorted to, it did injure the American importer, who had to produce the invoices from the manufacturer, showing the actual cost. The British manufacturer, however, could legitimately in-

[154] *Facts*, 1831, p. 13.
[155] *Facts*, 1831, p. 14.
[156] Niles, *Register*, 1819, vol. XV, p. 419.

voice his goods at a value lower than possible for the American importer, for his profit, reckoned at from ten to fifteen per cent on the cost, need not have been included in the invoice price.[157]

It was generally conceded that the placing of an agent in the United States to whom the British manufacturer or merchant might consign, gave him another advantage over the American firm, in that he was able to escape many of the expenses of a permanent establishment.

"A considerable portion of the goods sold at auction in the United States are on account of *foreigners* who ship them direct to the auctioneer, or to agents who place them in his hands, thus avoiding the expenses of warehouses, stores, and other parts of a mercantile establishment to which merchants in the regular line of business are subjected."[158]

What might be called unfair methods of competition seem to have placed the importer at a disadvantage. It was frequently asserted that if an American importer were to send an order to Great Britain for goods, the manufacturer or merchant would immediately duplicate the order on his own account. The struggles of the importer were described as follows:

"The American Importer continued to make attempts to import goods, but they were nearly always unsuccessful. How could it be otherwise when orders have been given to English manufacturers, and the same ship that brought the goods, has also brought from the same houses other similar parcels on their own account which were sent to the auction room almost before the importer had received the goods from the vessel."[159]

In a Memorial presented to Congress in 1820, it was stated that:

"Large consignments of merchandise are, also, made by foreign houses to their agents, and others, residing in this country, upon the information taken from American orders and commissions, after the American merchants had given their orders, to the full extent that it was safe and proper to be done; and many of the goods thus imported, being sold at public auction for cash, afford to the foreign owner the use of capital, equal to the amount and credit on the duties."[160]

[157] *Facts*, 1831, p. 12. For a general discussion of this topic, see Westerfield, *Auctions*, 1920, pp. 191-193.
[158] *Memorial of Chamber of Commerce of New York*, 1820 (32), p. 6.
[159] *Facts*, 1831, pp. 10-11.
[160] *Memorial of Merchants of Baltimore*, 1820 (30), p. 4.

The agents in America were always on the alert to anticipate orders sent to England. They were in constant attendance at the public sales; "numbers could be seen at public auctions, taking patterns and marking the prices . . . to be transmitted to England by the next packet."[161] A writer in Niles' *Register* explained that:

"It is the practice of these foreign adventurers to be always on the alert and to obtain copies of orders sent to England by the old and experienced American importers, and the articles directed by them to be furnished as suitable for our market, are hastily prepared and sent off to anticipate such orders, and supply the market before the goods on account of such orders shall reach the United States."[162]

The methods of paying the customs duties, which obtained at various times, were also considered by many writers of the time to give to the British consignor an advantage over the American importer. Until 1842 importers were allowed to enter goods without immediate payment of the duties, upon giving bonds for the payment of the duties within a certain period.[163] This was probably necessary at a time when commercial capital was not abundant. That it was considered by some a desirable feature is shown in the Memorial submitted to Congress in 1820 by the Salem merchants. They argued that when a voyage was to be undertaken, much capital had to be invested in the vessel and the cargo, and a certain amount allowed for the expenses of the voyage. On the return of the vessel the goods imported could not be sold immediately; and the sales which were made were rarely for cash.[164] Under these circumstances the credits on the duties, which varied from three months to twelve months, according to the commodity and the country from which it was imported, were felt to be essential to the well being of the commercial class, and the merchants in question accordingly opposed a change to cash payments. The Memorial stated that:

". . . if a cash payment is required for the duties, it is obvious that the merchant must either, in anticipation of this demand, gradually withdraw from his other business a portion of the capital equal to the duties, or he must divert an equal portion ready to be employed in an-

---

161 *Facts*, 1831, p. 9.
162 Niles, *Register*, 1825, vol. XXVII, p. 289.
163 Dewey, *Financial History of the United States*, 1912, p. 239.
164 *Salem Memorial*, 1820, p. 12.

other voyage; or he must procure money on credit from other sources; or he must consent to make enormous sacrifices by an immediate forced sale."[165]

But this viewpoint was not general, at least at the time when the auction system was considered a menace to the interests of the importing merchant. The merchant believed that a potent cause of the success of the competition he had to face was the credit which was allowed on the duties. A writer, complaining of this inducement offered to the consignor, estimated that a British agent at New York could make three importations before the duties on the first goods imported became due. He said:

"Thus a British agent at New York imports $1,000 worth of goods—others of his country men sign the bonds at the custom house, and the goods pass from the ship to the auction room; then, as the duties will average 33 1-3d per cent if the goods are only sold at cost and charges, the agent receives $1,333.33 for them,—which are sent off for fresh supplies—and as the average run of the bonds is 10 months, ample time is allowed for three importations, and the 1,000 dollars of British capital is increased to 2,000 dollars."[166]

The extent to which the customs regulations facilitated the importation of articles of commerce is shown in the following example:

"A cargo of teas, arriving in this country, to a favorable market and immediately sold will furnish the means, both as to time and amount, for a new voyage of equal value, by the credit alone which is allowed for the payment of the duties, without the aid of any other capital. A cargo of West India spirits, arriving and being sold, under the same circumstances, will furnish, in like manner, the means of two subsequent voyages, the second double the amount of the first, before the expiration of the credit on the duties."[167]

It is probable that too much emphasis was laid on the influence which credits on duties played in encouraging the British consignors. There was no differentiation between the imports on British and on American account. Either had the privilege of giving bonds for the payment of the duties, and hence the use of the funds during the same period. Possibly in one way the

---

[165] *Memorial of the Merchants . . . in Salem*, 1820, p. 11.

[166] Niles, *Register*, 1828, vol. XXXIV, p. 106.

[167] *Memorial of the Merchants of Baltimore*, 1820 (30), p. 4. *Facts*, 1831, p. 9.

British agent was placed in a superior position to the American importer. If the payment of the duties became necessary before the goods were sold, he could more easily secure the necessary funds with which to settle for them, for he could draw a draft on his principal in England which was readily discounted, while the American importer had to borrow funds from his bank or some other source.

It is a curious fact that whatever system of paying the customs duties was in force or was advocated at any time, there were some who saw in it the reason for the suppression of the American importer. A writer of a later period objected to the payment of duties in cash on the ground that it would tend to throw the business into the hands of the European houses, and, as between American houses, would favor the large capitalist as against the small.

"A large portion of the import trade in foreign manufactures has always been in the hands of European houses, and the payment of the duties in cash has the tendency to throw a still larger portion of it into their control; for they are not only generally capitalists, who, without inconvenience, can advance the duty, but they also have the facility of doing it by their agents drawing on their principals in Europe, which bills can be covered previous to maturity from the proceeds of the sale, while the American importer is obliged to raise the amount at a higher rate of interest; and frequently at a sacrifice; and even as between resident American houses, it acts to the disadvantage of the small, and in favour of the large capitalist."[168]

168 Hunt, *Merchants' Magazine,* 1846, XIV, p. 151.

The possible divergence of opinion on the effects of a particular system of revenue collection is illustrated by two reports of Committees of the House of Representatives, one in 1837 and the other in 1843. The first report is advocating the introduction of the warehousing system, and criticising the Tariff Act of 1832, which somewhat changed the credit period. The report stated:

"The two sections referred to [secs. 5 and 6] in effect impose cash duties, not only on wool and woolens, but upon merchandise of every description. The importer is required to advance the first installment of the duty to the government in most cases before the merchandise is demanded for consumption, or his property must, in three months, be sacrificed by a forced sale at public auction for cash. With a very moderate rate of duty, the evils resulting from the execution of these provisions might be tolerated; but, with the high duties now prevailing, every enterprising merchant of limited capital must be driven out of the business of importing, commission houses will be compelled to refuse consignments of dutiable articles, and many

Later in the nineteenth century, when the warehousing system was in operation, it was maintained by the House Committee on Manufactures that this system was the main cause of the successful competition of the foreign merchant. The report asserted:

"The conviction is irresistibly forced upon the Committee, that we owe it mainly to the warehousing system that the American importers, who made the name of merchant honorable, have been to a great extent driven from the field, and that the business of importing foreign manufactured goods has mainly become a mere shipment of products from the factory abroad to agents here, who sell the goods for commission and send the proceeds to the foreign owner."[169]

branches of our foreign trade will be thrown exclusively into the hands of foreign houses, by the unequal operation of our own laws. The foreign importer may permit his merchandise to remain three months in the public store, then send bills on his partner abroad, at ninety days sight, for the amount of the duty, and thus avail himself of a credit equal to about seven months; while merchandise of the American importer of limited capital, must generally be sold at public auction at the expense both of his capital and credit." (H. R., 195, 24th Cong., 2d Sess., 1837, p. 3. Report of Committee of Ways and Means on Warehouse System. The sections of the tariff of 1832 referred to in the above quotation provided for cash payment of duties on wool and woolens, and payment of other duties, one-half in three months, and one-half in six months. *Cf.* Bolles, *Financial History,* 1885, p. 495.)

The committee which reported in 1843 on complaints similar to the one presented above did not believe that the system of credits then in operation had the influence popularly ascribed to it. It claimed that fully half of the goods imported paid no duties at all, that in the majority of cases the goods which were dutiable were sold before the credits of three and six months had expired, and concluded that the method of collecting the duties was not responsible for the situation of the American importer. (H. R., 103, 27th Cong., 3d Sess., 1843, p. 8. Report from Committee on Commerce on Warehouse System.) The view which it stated on this point follows:

"It is a prevailing impression, which seems to be well supported by facts, that the American market has been greatly disturbed by the influx of large amounts of foreign merchandise thrown into it, chiefly from England, France and Germany, upon foreign consignment, under circumstances requiring early sales at auction, without regard to any fixed rate of profit—even in view of certain loss—for the sake of speedy remittances of the proceeds; that these consignments, being often the surplus stocks of the nations from which they came, were made without calculation of gain and were sent to this country only because it is deemed more to the interest of the nation producing a surplus to dispose of it in a foreign market than in its own." (H. R., 103, 27th Cong., 3d Sess., 1843, p. 7. Report from Committee on Commerce on Warehouse System.)

[169] H. R., 67, 40th Cong., 2d Sess., June 22, 1868, pp. 29-30. Report from Committee on Manufactures.

It is not believed that such explanations can really get at the fundamental facts in the situation. Methods of custom entry may, it is true, favor the citizen of one country over another, but the custom laws of the United States paid no attention to the ownership of the goods, whatever its policy may have been with respect to the nationality of the vessel. The success which so long attended the foreign consignor in his competition with the American importing merchant must have rested on deeper economic grounds.

The real underlying cause of this success, and the basis of the long-continued competition is believed to be connected with the change in the methods of production in England. The introduction of the factory system, bringing about as it did some of the economies of large-scale production, and making possible the reduction of the unit cost of manufacturing, constantly spurred the manufacturers who were in competition with each other to increase the size and efficiency of their plants. Each one wished to secure for himself the profits which were possible if he could sell at the ruling market price, and at the same time lower his costs per unit by increasing his production.

America presented a very favorable dumping ground for excess production. The manufacturers may have hesitated to reduce the price in England, but the goods had to be disposed of, and hence they were sent to America and other foreign countries to be sold at auction. The American importer was virtually attempting to compete with British manufacturers engaged in cutthroat competition with each other. It is not at all remarkable that he found difficulty in purchasing in England at prices which would yield him a profit when sold in America; the British manufacturer tried to maintain his prices in the home market.

Another view of the difficulty the American merchant found confronting him was that this ruthless competition was a well-calculated effort on the part of the British merchants and manufacturers to stifle the recently established manufactures of America. That this belief was held by the mercantile class of America is apparent. A speech of Mr. Brougham, in which references to such a policy occurred, was given considerable publicity, and tended to lead to a conviction that a conspiracy was on foot to destroy the American manufactures. The passage referred to follows:

". . . it was worth while to incur a loss upon the first exportations in order, by the glut, to stifle in the cradle those rising manufactures in the United States which the war had forced into existence contrary to the natural course of things."[170]

A writer, speaking of the agents of the British in the United States who received consignments from manufacturers and merchants in Great Britain, claimed to have no doubt that "they are agents of the British government or of a combination of manufacturers who are willing to sacrifice a considerable sum to suppress our manufacturing establishments."[171] Again in the next year we find this statement:

"It appears to us now to be a well established fact that rich and extensive associations have been formed in Great Britain and large sums of money subscribed for the purpose of putting down American manufactures. The association seems to have agreed to sacrifice the sum of 300,000£ sterling (1,332,000 dollars) in the experiment, to inundate our country with goods and dispose of them on any terms which may best have effect on our establishments; believing that when these are once destroyed, they may hold the market at their own prices."[172]

Further confirmation of a belief in a hostile program deliberately adopted and carried out by the British capitalists is given by the following quotation from a Memorial submitted to Congress in 1819:

"It is well known, and we presume cannot have escaped the knowledge of Congress, that, at all times, under all circumstances, and at every hazard of expense, the government, merchants, and manufacturers of Great Britain, have their views steadily directed to the extirpation of every germ of manufactures among us."[173]

It was doubtless true that manufacturers who were forced to incur a loss on the goods sold in the American market found some comfort in the fact that the destruction of the rising manufacturing establishments would improve the market in the future. And possibly some manufacturers did consciously adopt this policy, but no evidence has been found which indicates the existence of combinations on the part of the manufacturers with this end in view.

[170] Niles, *Register*, 1817, vol. II, p. 284, quoted from a speech in Parliament. See Hansard, *Parl. Debates*, 1st Series, XXXIII, 1099.
[171] *Ibid.*, 1819, vol. XV, p. 419.
[172] *Ibid.*, 1820, vol. XVIII, p. 151.
[173] *Memorial . . . of New York*, 1819 (9), p. 7.

SUMMARY AND CONCLUSIONS

The sale of consigned goods at auction did for a considerable period of time so circumscribe the operations of the American importing merchant that he was a negligible factor in the commerce between America and Great Britain, except in so far as he acted as consignee for goods. Always frowned upon, and often the subject of violent attacks by merchants,[174] the auction maintained its position without serious interference, probably because of the elemental fact that it provided goods for the ordinary consumer more cheaply than the importing merchants could have done.[175] It served to introduce new goods, it assisted in forming new tastes on the part of the consumer, and it forced the importing merchants, who could still maintain themselves

---

[174] There were numerous complaints made of the abuses and evils connected with the auction system, probably largely because of the fact that it tended to eliminate the American merchant as an independent importer. Many petitions were presented to Congress praying for legislation to curb the auction, and practically every petition enumerated the evils resulting therefrom. It was alleged, for example, that the goods were flimsy in texture, that the dyes were spurious, that the names and marks of well known manufacturers were counterfeited, that textiles were sold at short measure and the auctioneers would not allow for shortage except within such a short time that it was impossible to examine the goods. (*Facts*, 1831, pp. 15-25.) A typical example of such charges is given in the following extract from a Memorial to Congress in 1819:

"Large quantities of silk, woollen, cotton and other goods are manufactured in Europe and the East Indies expressly for sale at auction in the United States. These goods are of less than the usual length, deficient in breadth, of a flimsy texture; in short, inferior in every respect to the goods they are intended to represent; yet, so well dressed, and in other respects, so highly finished to the eye, that they generally escape detection till they reach the consumer, who too late discovers their inferiority." (*Memorial*, 1819 (9), p. 8.)

Doubtless many of these charges were well founded, but it should be remembered that the individuals of public bodies making them were not at all disinterested, but were attempting to secure the enactment of restrictive legislation.

For a full account of the complaints against the auction, see Westerfield, *Auctions*, 1920, pp. 193-198.

[175] The chief advantage of auction claimed for it by the auctioneers was that it tended to place goods in the hands of consumers at a lower price. (Westerfield, *Auctions*, 1920, p. 182.) On the other hand, it was often alleged that this advantage was quite illusive, as it was claimed that the lower price was given at the expense of quality.

"Though goods are sometimes sold very cheap at auctions, we must always keep in mind that the constant tendency of auctions is to *deteriorate*

in business, to the greatest degree of efficiency, while it probably introduced into the domestic merchandising system elements of competition and of economy which had never been known before.

While speculation in business was probably fostered by the auction system it made for progress, and in our judgment there is little question that it justified its existence when viewed from the standpoint of society, and not of the individual.

the quality. When this is taken into account, there can be no doubt that purchasers pay more for our goods than they do at private sale.'' (*Facts*, 1831, p. 29.)

It was also asserted that for the same quality of goods a higher price could be obtained at auction than at private sale. (Niles, *Register*, 1829, vol. XXXVI, p. 186.)

CHAPTER VII

THE TRADE IN BRITISH MANUFACTURES, 1830-1850

THE organisation of the export trade of Great Britain around the year 1830 presented a singularly complicated aspect. There were many agents and agencies engaged in the task of purchasing or conveying the manufactures to the different markets of the world. A rather vivid picture of the situation at this time was given by an American in a communication to the *Liverpool Mercury*.

" 'The persons engaged in obtaining and vending the manufactures of this country are very various—Commission merchants, who reside in manufacturing towns, and receive orders to purchase on foreign account, being furnished with letters of credit on mercantile houses in this country, or with bills of exchange; partners of houses abroad who purchase and sell on their own account; persons provided with funds to advance on consignments—manufacturers who consign their goods for sale on commission or thru agents sent out;—the manufacturers who send out goods to persons abroad dividing profit and loss;—merchants who purchase and consign for sale on commission.' "[176]

Of these different methods described the most important from the standpoint of volume of goods handled continued to be the system of consignment by a manufacturer or merchant to an agent in America, who put them up for sale in the auction room. In a report published as late as 1869 it was estimated that at least sixty per cent of the textile fabrics and fancy goods imported into the United States were consignments from needy manufacturers or commercial speculators in Europe, and were destined to be sold, many of them, at auction.

"Investigation renders it probable that at least sixty per cent of the textile fabrics and fancy goods which are entered in warehouses are not *bona fide* purchases. Investigation further shows that needy manu-

[176] *Liverpool Mercury*, March 2, 1832, p. 72. Quoted from letter signed "New York," dated February 29, 1832 (and hence written in England).

facturers in Europe, or commercial adventurers in the possession of goods, often very undesirable articles, apply to numerous foreign houses who have agents in the United States, for advances, and then consign them to this country, . . . Now such a trade is clearly detrimental to the *bona-fide* merchant, and rarely a benefit to the consumer, inasmuch as the goods which are sold at auction, if desirable, are retailed at regular prices; and if undesirable, are no benefit to any one."[177]

In times of business depression manufacturers who ordinarily may have disposed of their goods by sale to merchants added to the volume of consignments, for they preferred to sell their surplus production at a low price in a foreign market rather than to reduce the price at their own warehouses.

"It happens however . . . that immense amounts of foreign goods are often poured into the United States, upon the great points of importation, under circumstances of commercial pressure and distress, producing great disturbances, and fluctuation of prices. At such periods, the manufacturers, if pressed for money, instead of at once reducing the price of goods at their warehouses . . . generally prefer to make sacrifices of their surplus stock at distant points—they sometimes ship to foreign ports and sell by their own agents, on their own account, in which case they can lessen the duties by making out their invoices at lower rates . . .; they sometimes make loans from mercantile houses having branches in other countries, and deposit their surplus goods as security, upon the agreement that they are to be sold for whatever they will bring, to refund the advances, if they are not paid when due. Great quantities of these goods, and also of failing merchants are thrown upon the Northern markets, especially New York, and sold at auction for whatever they will bring. . . ."[178]

The system of consignments and sale by auction nevertheless had declined relatively in importance. A larger proportion of the imports were made by the American importer on his own account than earlier, and we hear fewer complaints of the auction system by the merchants. Westerfield notes that in the decade from 1830 to 1840 the auction played a less important rôle than it had previously, and became less offensive to the commercial class.

"Steam navigation brought together the agents of foreign commission houses and the jobbers of this country and the inducements for a

[177] House Ex. Doc. §16, 40th Cong., 3d Sess., January 5, 1869. Report of Special Commissioner of the Revenue (David A. Wells), p. 82.

[178] DeBow, *Review*, 1847, IV, p. 495.

speculative and uncertain market were lessened. The introduction of the bond and warehouse system enabled importers to hold their surplus stocks from auction until the market could absorb them in the regular mode of private sales. Many articles which were previously sold largely at auction either ceased to be imported on account of our rising manufactures, or for other reasons, or came to be largely sold through brokers. It seems that the auction duties proved prohibitive in case of certain commodities and these were increasingly sold through brokers. By 1844, at least, the anti-auction war had passed and the era of peace prevailed."[179]

THE AMERICAN IMPORTING MERCHANT

From 1830 on the American importer quite noticeably became a figure of greater importance in the Anglo-American trade. He was a purchaser of goods himself, and not merely a consignee of goods from the British merchant or manufacturer.

We have noted that in the years before 1812 certain American importing merchants had been accustomed to send agents to England, or to go to England themselves, to select the goods which they desired. In all probability a few continued this custom during the second period, but certainly it was not a widespread practice. Somewhere around the year 1830—it is impossible to determine the exact date—American importers in large numbers again began to make their purchases in Great Britain in person. This struck the attention of the Parliamentary Committee investigating the state of the manufactures in 1833, and they asked Mr. Bates, a member of Baring Brothers and Company, and active in American trade for many years, if a practice had not grown up of late years which had not existed before, of the Americans coming over themselves to see the goods and make their purchases. Mr. Bates replied that he believed that that practice had always existed, and then stated that "they generally have a partner upon this side to superintend their purchases."[180]

James, who wrote in 1857, noted this increase in the number of foreign merchants resident in England, and, although he did not specifically mention American merchants as being of their number, it does not seem unreasonable to assume that some of those of whom he spoke were Americans.

". . . many foreign merchants, who previously employed agents, or

[179] Westerfield, *Auctions*, 1920, p. 208.
[180] Parl. Papers, Report on Manufactures, 1833, p. 61.

obtained their supplies from consignments to them by English merchants, began to settle in the worsted districts of the West-Riding. This circumstance undoubtedly had a great influence upon the prosperity of our export trade, for the foreign merchants being on the spot, could not only avail themselves of any advantages which offered in the market, but also stimulated the manufacturers to make, in the best manner, fabrics suited for the respective continental markets. . . . These merchants at the time I write, are a large and respectable colony in Bradford;"[181]

An American source gives us the same testimony—that after 1830 the number of American merchants in Great Britain had increased to a considerable degree.

"A large part of the manufactures of Great Britain imported into the United States have for some years past been purchased of the manufacturers by agents of the American importers residing in England. . . ."[182]

Further confirmation of the growing importance of the American importing merchant is given in the following quotation from an article appearing in 1837:

". . . the increase of trade . . . gradually introduced, and ultimately established, a more convenient and cheaper, but far less safe mode of carrying on the trade. This was brought about by the importing houses in America establishing agents in the manufacturing districts of this country, and also in the Continent, China, etc., for the purchase and shipment of products for the United States."[183]

Another writer, of a somewhat later date, spoke of the American importer "on his own account, with partner and house in England, probably of substance, as he may be, and of credit as he is," as if it were quite the normal thing for the importer to deal directly with the British markets through his own foreign branch.[184]

The operations of the American importer were much facilitated by the extension of the banking and credit system of Great Britain, and particularly of London. Of course, payments for exports and imports had for a long period been effected through the medium of bills of exchange, but it was in this period

181 James, *History of Worsted Manufacture*, 1857, p. 411.
182 *Financial Register*, 1838, I, p. 274.
183 *Edinburgh Review*, 1837, vol. LXVII, no. 132, p. 229.
184 *Bankers' Magazine* (London), 1854, XIV, p. 606.

that we find the establishment in the United States of branches
or agents of merchants and bankers of Great Britain, with authority to grant letters of credit to merchants about to send
abroad for a cargo.[185]

An American merchant who wished to purchase goods through
his agent, resident in Great Britain, could therefore secure from
the agent of one of these large Anglo-American houses a letter
of credit, giving him the right to draw a bill, usually at four
months, on the house in London. The London office of the house
accepted the bill when presented, and paid it when due, with the
understanding that the American merchant should provide the
local agent or the London office with the necessary means to
meet the bill at maturity. A British writer in 1838 thus described this method of carrying on the foreign trade:

"There are at present many houses in England who have partners or
agents in America, and the American merchant, wishing to order goods
from England, arranges with these parties as follows: He pays into
their hands ten or twenty per cent, as may be agreed upon, of the
amount of goods he intends to order, and obtains authority to draw, or
cause to be drawn, upon the house in England, bills at four months, for
the amount of the goods purchased; he then either comes himself to
England or sends his orders to some agent, to make his purchases for
him."[186]

William Brown, of the house of Brown Brothers and Company, in 1847 gave testimony showing that at that date also the
British banking and commercial houses were financing the operations of American importers.

"Mr. A. in the United States goes to my brother, my partner in
America, and states that he wants to import £1000 or £2000 value of
goods. They look into the credit of the house, and if they are satisfied,
a Credit is opened with us. The order goes to the manufacturing districts, to some individual who is authorized by us, when the goods are
ready, to draw upon us for the Amount of this Credit."[187]

At first it was customary for the bills of lading and the invoices to be sent to the agents of the accepting house in America
in order to give it security for the ultimate fulfillment of the
contract by the American merchant.

185 *North American Review*, 1844, vol. LVIII, p. 111.
186 Joplin, *Banking*, 1838, p. 42.
187 Parl. Papers, Report on Commercial Distress, 1847-1848, vol. XXIV
(31), p. 262.

"The goods being purchased and drawn for, are shipped to America; not to the American merchant, but to the partner or agent of the house who has accepted the bill for them, and he turns them over to the American merchant, upon receiving good bills upon London for the balance, over and above the sum first deposited; and should the American merchant not fulfill his contract, the London house is at liberty to sell the goods and pay themselves, charging the loss to the American merchant."[188]

This method of conducting business was profitable to all concerned; to the British manufacturer, because he received a bill of exchange which could be turned into cash immediately; to the American importer, because he got the benefit of lower prices for prompt payments; and to the British banking house, which received a commission for accepting the bills of exchange, without having advanced any actual funds.

It was, moreover, not only a profitable arrangement, but an eminently safe one. The creation of bills of exchange depended on actual commercial transactions and these bills were self-liquidating in the majority of cases.

This conservatism did not long endure, and even in the thirties we find overconfidence, and competition among the houses for the American trade, leading them to send the invoices and bills of lading directly to the importers in America, leaving in the hands of the bankers no concrete security covering the amounts for which they had accepted.

"It seemed to be unnecessary to require any such collateral security [bills of lading, etc.] from American houses of undoubted wealth and known prudence in the conduct of their affairs; and if one English house thought this was unnecessary in the case of Messrs. A. of New York, another thought it unnecessary in the case of Messrs. B. of Boston, and so on; till at length the practice was in all cases resisted by the Americans as illiberal and invidious, and abandoned by the English as useless."[189]

As might have been expected, this liberal credit policy opened the way for abuses and speculation. Importing houses in America secured credits with a number of different houses as a means of raising money, and as a bill on one house became due they settled for it by a bill on another house.[190]

---

[188] Joplin, *Banking*, 1838, p. 42. *Cf.* also quotation from this author, p. 155.

[189] *Edinburgh Review*, 1837, vol. LXVII, no. 132, p. 230.

[190] *Financial Register*, 1838, I, p. 274.

"It appears that a large portion of these bills, instead of being based on *bona fide* security lodged in the hands of the bankers upon whom they were drawn, were drawn for what is called by merchants, *blank credits*,—they were bills drawn upon open credits, with the understanding that they should be provided for at maturity. . . .

"The parties in America, not content with carrying on business and possessing credit with one house only, appear to have had these large transactions and open credits with many London houses, and to have used in succession the credit on one house for the purpose of paying the debt due to another.

"Thus a constant succession of bills was provided on a credit basis, and one house was paid by drafts on the other. These houses were not aware of the hollowness of their own connexion. Each supposed that the drafts represented regular business, presuming his neighbour to be more prudent than himself."[191]

The results of this practice added considerably to the embarrassments of 1837, when three of the large banking houses were forced to stop payment because of the failure of American firms to provide funds with which to meet drafts at maturity. The action of the Bank of England in refusing to rediscount the drafts drawn on these three Anglo-American houses tended to curb the speculative dealings, and confine the business to more legitimate channels.

It is interesting to note that the financing of American trade was confined largely to about seven houses, six in London and one in Liverpool. They did an enormous business; at certain periods of 1835 and 1836 they were estimated to have acceptances outstanding amounting to fifteen or sixteen million pounds sterling.[192] Their capital resources were very large, so large in fact that except in times of financial stringency they did not find it necessary to rediscount with the Bank of England or the discount brokers any of the bills which they received.[193]

During the panic of 1837 three of these houses, as noted above, stopped payment. These were the firms of T. Wilson and Company, T. Wiggin and Company, and G. Wildes and Company— known generally as the three "W's." A letter of Wiggin and Company indicated the general nature of their business in 1837. They were purely bankers: "no part of it [the liabilities] was

191 Salomons, *Monetary Difficulties of America,* 1837, p. 23.
192 *Edinburgh Review,* 1837, vol. LXVII, no. 132, p. 231.
193 Joplin, *Banking,* 1838, p. 43.

on our own account, nor have we owned any merchandise whatever since we commenced business; consequently the bills accepted by us were for account of others, who owed, and still owe, so far as they remain unpaid.'' The liabilities were said to be entirely for advances on consignments of merchandise to the United States, not alone from England, but also from China, India, and other parts of the world.[194]

Brown Brothers and Company, another firm largely engaged in banking, was also in business as a commission merchant. It not only received produce for sale in Liverpool, but also facilitated the shipments of goods to the United States, and lodged credits all over the world for other establishments, thus assisting in the financing of various phases of American foreign trade.[195] Many of these firms combined banking and commerce, and probably most of them began their careers as merchants, and then gradually developed the financial end of the business.

These houses served the Americans not only in their trade with Great Britain, but in their trade with other lands as well. It had long been customary and necessary for a merchant sending a vessel to India, or China, or to South America, to ship specie with which to procure a part of the return cargo. This specie eventually found its way back to London, or to cities where it came under the control of the bankers of London. That this was an uneconomical method of paying for goods is obvious, and the Anglo-American houses offered facilities which made trading to these far ports both safer and less expensive. By means of a credit opened in the United States with one of these houses, a merchant could draw a bill of exchange on London and tender it, for example, in payment for cotton goods from Canton.[196]

In settlement of the claims thus created against the American importer, bills of exchange drawn against exports of produce from America to Great Britain or to the Continent were remitted. Merchants of doubtful credit might be required to furnish acceptable bills of exchange before a credit was opened, but it was not customary to remit earlier than necessary to protect

[194] *Financial Register*, 1837, I, pp. 233, 241. Joplin, *Banking*, 1838, p. 47.
[195] Parl. Papers, Report on Commercial Distress, 1847-1848, vol. XXIV (31), p. 253.
[196] *North American Review*, 1844, vol. LVIII, p. 111-112. *Financial Register*, 1837, I, p. 274.

the accepting bank or merchant when the bill fell due. The *Liverpool Mercury* says of this practice:

"To an inexperienced person it would appear that a purchaser of goods here for bills on his merchant, had left with him produce on which account he was drawing. This is not generally the case; he draws on credit, and his bills are to be retired by remittances from the other side, after the arrival of the goods out. The transaction is considered commercial; the merchant charges one per cent for accepting."[197]

THE BRITISH EXPORTING MERCHANT

Goods were purchased by British merchants, acting for themselves or for clients, in much the same way as by American agents. Bills of exchange, running from four to six months, were given in exchange for the goods.[198] A witness before the committee on commercial distress in 1847 thus described the business methods in use in Lancashire.

". . . the mode of conducting business is this, the manufacturers in Lancaster sell to the Manchester houses at four months; they sell this month, and the goods are paid for the next, and the buyers have the option of paying in Bank of England notes, and deducting interest at five per cent, or paying in a three months' bill."[199]

The allowance of a discount of five per cent for payments in cash made it worth while for the merchant to discount his note when the rate of discount was lower than five per cent; otherwise it was to his interest to pay by a bill of exchange.[200] The merchant in possession of a trade acceptance was enabled, if he so chose, to secure cash at once by discounting it with one of the discount brokers, or the banking houses. These in turn could then, as now, rely on the Bank of England for rediscounts. The Bank of England was somewhat more stringent in its rules regarding the term of the bill of exchange than the note brokers and the other discounting houses, for it usually refused to rediscount notes or bills exceeding ninety-five days. It did, however, make temporary loans on bills which had not more than

---

[197] *Liverpool Mercury*, March 2, 1832, p. 72.

[198] Slack, *Commercial Caution*, 1835, p. 16.

[199] Parl. Papers, Report on Commercial Distress, 1847-1848, vol. XXVII (213), p. 473. *Cf.* also *ibid.*, vol. XXIV (31), p. 243.

[200] Parl. Papers, Report on Commercial Distress, 1847-1848, vol. XXVII (213), p. 3.

six months to run. The loans were repayable before the bills matured, and the bills were therefore considered as collateral security only.[201]

AMERICAN CREDIT RELATIONS

The New York importer did not as a general rule deal directly with the country merchant. He imported in bales and packages, and sold in bales and packages,—quantities too large for country merchants. There was a certain specialisation among importers, so that there were almost as many distinct classes of importers as there were different classes of goods; hence the country merchant was unable to secure a variety of goods from the importer. Assortments of various goods in quantities to suit the country merchants could be secured from another type of merchant called the jobber. The jobbers bought from the importers in bales and packages, and broke these into convenient lots for sale to the country merchant or dealer. The jobber was the regular customer of the importing merchant, and if an importer did sell to the country merchant, it was for cash or on terms which would not constitute competition with the jobber.[202]

Even late in the first half of the nineteenth century the credit was very long. The jobber paid for the goods he purchased with a note running from six to eight months. He sold the goods to the country merchant on similar terms, and the country merchant was forced to "trust" the planter or the farmer for perhaps a longer time.[203] There is evidence to show that some credits ran for longer than eight months. Lee, in 1843, wrote of longer credits as characteristic of New England.

"This system, *peculiar to New England,* of trusting out nearly all the products of her industry on credit averaging eight to twelve months, and perhaps twelve to fifteen months, before payments are made, while we are compelled to pay *cash* for all the goods we buy south of the Hudson—*is the worst feature in the commercial and manufacturing policy of New England.*"[204]

In the South the credits were said to be much longer than in New York. Elmore, writing in DeBow's *Review,* said:

"In Charleston, during the past season, the credits given by the

[201] Parl. Papers, Report on Commercial Distress, 1847-1848, vol. XXVII (213), p. 272. Testimony of Governor of Bank.

[202] DeBow, *Review,* 1847, IV, p. 497.

[203] *Ibid.,* p. 499; Parl. Papers, Report on Manufactures, 1833, p. 170.

[204] Lee, *Cotton Letters,* p. 51.

wholesale merchants have gone from six to twelve months, averaging perhaps nine or ten months. The medium of payments is not less important—payments in New York are by banknotes at a discount, or exchange at a premium. In Charleston the committee are informed that the banknotes of most of the Southern States are taken at par, constituting a saving of from one to three per cent."[205]

The question presents itself as to whether the system of dealing on credit increased or decreased during the period, and whether the time given for payment of goods tended to lengthen or be shortened. Our evidence is far too meagre to allow us to generalise on this point. Such evidence as we have, however, points towards an extension of the credit system and the credit period. Lee noted the unsound basis on which credits were granted.

"Under an extreme credit system, as in this country, where goods to a heavy amount are sold on the security of a single name, for eight, ten and twelve months, and to persons whose trading capital in a majority of cases, is nothing *but mere credit,* there can be no great difficulty in disposing of any quantity, so long as there are banks that will cash the notes given in payment."[206]

Again he claimed that the period of credit had lengthened from about four months to twelve months.

"The abuse of the credit system has been mainly owing to the ambitious views of wealthy and enterprising importers and commission houses in New York and elsewhere, of men who were desirous of engrossing an undue share of business—an object which could only be accomplished by tempting enterprising and sanguine men into dealings with them, and beyond their ordinary purchases—by the offers of long terms of credit. It was the effect of this imprudent system, aided as it was by an extension of bank credits, from the former ones of two, three, four months to six, nine, and twelve months, and those credits and loans founded upon any kind of securities, whether based on property or not."[207]

In 1839 a notice appeared in the *New Orleans Price Current,* signed by many of the commission merchants and factors of New Orleans who were handling western produce, to the effect that an additional charge of two and one-half per cent would be made on all sales effected on credit. The reason assigned for this

[205] DeBow, *Review,* 1847, IV, p. 499.
[206] Lee, *Cotton Letters,* p. 20.
[207] *Ibid.,* p. 53.

step was that so much more of the business was being done on credit than formerly that it was necessary in self-protection. They said:

"The system of credit which has pervaded our country generally of late years, but more especially our community of merchants, has wrought quite a change in the manner of transacting the produce business of this city, inasmuch as a very large portion of the vast amount of Western Produce disposed of here is now sold on time, whereas formerly it was entirely sold for cash."[208]

In view, however, of the long credits known to be customary about 1800, and in view of the fact that the capital accumulations of the country were increasing, there is reason to question such a conclusion as would be drawn from the statements above. While the speculative fever which seized all classes of people in the thirties probably did lead to an extension of the credit system, and to an overexpansion of the credit facilities, we are inclined to believe that the credit period probably was not extended to any marked degree.

CONCLUSIONS

The basic causes underlying the organisation of the export trade of Great Britain, and controlling its development are difficult to determine, and impossible to establish by direct evidence. We can, nevertheless, see some of the forces which were at work shaping and moulding the organisation; and at this point we wish to advance certain suggestions in explanation of the changes which, we have seen, took place in the methods of handling the exports of Great Britain.

The wide expansion of the factory system, and the production of textiles on a large scale, may be said to have resulted from the changes in the technique of production which formed such an important part of the Industrial Revolution. It is a fact, however, that these changes did not immediately destroy the domestic producer, or cause the concentration of all spinning and weaving in large factories. The transformation of the textile industries was a gradual process which was not complete in all lines even by 1850. In speaking of the persistence of the domestic system in the woolen industry, Lipson says:

"It is often assumed that the introduction of machinery forthwith

208 *New Orleans Price Current*, October 5, 1839.

created the factory system and extinguished the domestic system. This view needs to be very much qualified. The factory owners—for example, Benjamin Gott—undoubtedly made their appearance very early in the nineteenth century. They were recruited partly from the ranks of successful clothiers who bought machinery and started mills, but mainly from the class of merchants who were already responsible for the finishing processes, and now turned manufacturers, taking over from the clothier all the earlier processes. None the less, the domestic system held its ground successfully among 'the working clothiers' of the West Riding even beyond the middle of the nineteenth century, and as late as 1856 only about one-half of those engaged in the woollen industry in Yorkshire were employed in factories. The reasons for the survival of the domestic system in Yorkshire are two-fold. In the first place, the adoption of the power-loom in the woollen industry was very gradual. In 1835 Yorkshire contained only 688 power-looms for woollen weaving, or less than one-fourth of the number used in worsted weaving."[209]

Heaton, also writing of the woolen and worsted industries, calls attention to the fact that the full effects of the Industrial Revolution did not become manifest at once.

". . . the adoption of factory organisation and the introduction of machinery came very slowly. There were scarcely twenty factories in Yorkshire in 1800; the power-loom was not introduced into Bradford till 1826, when it was the cause of fierce strife and riots; combing was done by hand until well into the forties, and many technical difficulties rendered it undesirable to use the power-loom in the woollen industry until about 1850. . . . Thus we come to the conclusion that the Industrial Revolution had little more than its beginnings in the eighteenth century. . . . In the Yorkshire branches of the textile industry, the revolution did not actually take place until the nineteenth century; the face of Yorkshire had been little altered by 1800, and a half a century had still to elapse before it could be claimed that the factory and power-driven machinery had displaced the old hand methods."[210]

[209] Lipson, *History of Woollen and Worsted Industries*, 1921, p. 176.
The following are the figures for the number of worsted power-looms in West Riding:

Years	Number of Looms
1836	2,768
1841	11,458
1843	16,870
1845	19,121

Parl. Papers, Reports, 1845, vol. XXV, p. 437.
[210] Heaton, *Yorkshire Woollen and Worsted Industries*, 1920, p. 283.

In the cotton industry, changes came about more quickly than in the woolen and worsted industries, but even in this industry there was by no means a complete transformation by 1800. In fact, much later than 1800 we find that a large proportion of the cotton cloth was manufactured in relatively small factories or in the homes of the journeymen. A witness in 1821 asserted that a large proportion of the cotton goods were made by a journeyman working at the hand-loom in his own home.[211] As late as 1833 it was estimated that there were in the United Kingdom 200,000 hand-loom weavers of cotton,[212] and in the evidence in the report of 1834 it was stated that most of the cotton shipped from Glasgow to foreign parts was the product of the hand-loom.[213]

The manufacturers, in the period before 1815, were largely small manufacturers with moderate capital resources, and with a limited knowledge of the needs and possibilities of foreign markets.[214] It is true, as has been stated above, that in some districts there were the merchant-manufacturers—capitalists who combined manufacturing and merchandising, and who presumably had control of a greater amount of capital than the general run of small manufacturer. But in general the period of large-scale production had not come in by 1815.

The mercantile class, on the other hand, controlled relatively large quantities of capital; the transfer of capital to manufacturing, which was going on during and after this period, is evidence of this. They were able to assume marketing risks which the small manufacturer could not assume. Furthermore, they were men experienced in dealing with distant markets, they knew the ways of shipping, and the needs and capacities of the various foreign centres. Shipping in larger quantities than the manufacturer could, unless he acted as a merchant for others as well as for himself, the merchant could secure better freight rates, or could afford to ship the goods in his own vessels.

The situation in this period—1800-1815—is about what would naturally be expected. The risks of commerce were not so great as to make the merchant unwilling to assume them. The supply

---

[211] Parl. Papers, Report on Foreign Trade, 1821, VII (703), p. 19.
[212] Parl. Papers, Report on Manufactures, 1833, p. 566.
[213] Parl. Papers, Report on Hand-Loom Weavers, 1834, p. 109.
[214] Chapman, *Lancashire Cotton Industry*, 1904, p. 139.

of goods was increasing, but with the gradual lowering of the price of goods, the demand kept pace with the supply fairly well, and there seemed to be no danger of an extraordinary output, by a few manufacturers, ruining the market. The manufacturer was content to spend his time in making his goods—the work for which he was best fitted—while the merchant found a profitable outlet for his surplus capital in supporting the credit of the manufacturer while the goods were being sold.

The development of large-scale production brought about a somewhat different situation. When manufacturing is on a very small scale there is no general inducement for the producer to enlarge his output faster than the natural expansion of his resources will allow him. The economies in operation which result from large-scale production present, however, a constant incentive to increase the output, to speed up the productive processes. In other words, huge profits are possible if the manufacturer can lower his unit cost by increasing his output, and at the same time can sell the increased volume at the prevailing market price. When more than one producer feels this same stimulus to productive activity, the resulting increase in production will inevitably cause a fall in the price of the goods.

This transition from manufacturing on a small scale to manufacturing on a larger scale, which began before 1800, seems to have taken place to a greater degree after 1815. While the basic inventions in the cotton industry had been in use before 1815, and had indeed resulted in a great increase in the production of cotton yarn and cloth, the improvements in both the spinning and weaving machinery came after 1815, and strengthened the tendency towards the concentration of production in factories.[215] The increased volume of production testified to the growing use of improved machinery. The following table gives the official value of cotton manufactured goods exported from Great Britain from 1800 to 1833. Although it is not conclusive evidence of the proportion of the increase in production, yet it serves to indicate the enormous expansion of the cotton industry.

[215] Ellison, *Cotton Trade,* 1886, p. 59.

Official Value of Cotton Manufactures Exported from Great Britain.

Year ending June 5	Value of Exports
1800	£ 5,593,407
1805	7,834,564
1809	12,503,918
1810	18,425,614
1811	17,898,519
1812	11,529,551
1813	15,723,225
1814	records destroyed by fire
1815	16,535,528
1816	21,480,792
1817	16,183,975
1818	20,133,966
1819	21,292,354
1820	16,696,539
1825	27,171,556
1830	31,810,474[216]

We see in the first place that between 1800 and 1810 the value of the exports increased threefold, and it should be realised that the "official value" indicated the quantity exported and not the market value of the goods. From 1810 the value of the exports increased fairly steadily, until we find that about six times as much cotton cloth was exported in 1830 as in 1800.

In consequence of the duty imposed upon printed cottons it is possible to discover with considerable exactness the quantity of printed cottons produced at different periods up to 1831, when the duty was repealed. The table below gives the number of yards of cloth printed in Great Britain at different dates.

Yards of Cloth Printed in Great Britain.

Year	Yards
1796	20,621,797
1800	32,869,729
1814	124,613,472
1830	347,450,299[217]

[216] *Accounts and Papers,* 1830-1831, vol. X (145), p. 398.
[217] Porter, *Progress of the Nation,* 1912, p. 305.

These figures are rather illuminating in showing the increase in production which was made possible by improved methods, but they do not necessarily prove that there was a tendency towards the factory method of production, although it is true that the effective use of the new machinery depended somewhat on the factory system. In order to demonstrate this conclusively, statistics showing for different dates the number of cotton or textile factories and the average number of workers in each would be required. Such figures have not been found, but the evidence which we shall adduce indicates, if it does not prove, the transition from the domestic system to the factory system of manufacture after 1815.

On the next page is given an estimate of the number of operatives in the different branches of the cotton industry at different dates. The relatively small number of weavers in 1819-1821 is noteworthy. As the period advanced, the number of weavers in mills increased, and the number of hand-loom weavers decreased, until by 1860 it was considered to be too insignificant to record. The number of operatives in spinning mills was large even in 1819, but it also increased considerably during the period.

Number and Wages of Operatives in the Cotton Industry.

	1819-21	Wages Per Week s. d.	1829-31	Wages Per Week s. d.	1844-46	Wages Per Week s. d.	1859-61	Wages Per Week s. d.
Operatives in spinning mills	110,000	10 3	140,000	10 6	190,000	11 0	248,000	12 6
Operatives in weaving mills	10,000	9 6	50,000	9 6	150,000	10 0	203,000	11 10
Hand-loom weavers	240,000	8 0	225,000	7 0	60,000	8 0	......	..
Other operatives, bleachers, printers, dyers, etc.	85,000	10 3	100,000	10 6	140,000	11 0	195,000	12 6
Total	445,000		515,000		540,000		646,000	
Average		9 0		8 8		10 5		12 4[218]

218 Ellison, *Cotton Trade*, 1886, p. 66.

Another suggestion of the growing importance of the factory method of production is seen in the table below, which gives the number of cotton mills at work in Manchester and Salford for a number of different years, showing an increase from 1820 to 1832 in the number of factories of about forty-five per cent.

Number of Cotton Mills at Work in the Townships of Manchester and Salford, in Different Years.

Year	Number
1820	 66
1822	 72
1826	 92
1829	 95
1832	. . . . 96[219]

At the same time that the volume of cotton goods was increasing, there was a decline both in the price of the goods and in the price of raw cotton. The following table gives the prices of raw cotton and of a certain grade of cotton cloth for selected years, together with the percentages of change in price.

Average Prices of Cotton and Cotton Cloth.

Year	One Piece of Calico at Manchester			Uplands Middling at Liverpool, per lb.	
	s.	d.	%	d.	%
1816	16	8½	271	18¼	215
1820	12	1½	197	11½	135
1825	8	5¼	137	11⅝	137
1830	6	3¼	102	6⅞	81
1833	6	2	100	8½	100[220]

The prices of cotton cloth and of raw cotton did not decline at the same rate; between 1816 and 1833 the price of cotton cloth dropped much more rapidly than the price of cotton. This would seem to point to economies in operation, the result of operations on a larger scale, because we find that the wages of the workers did not drop during the period, but tended rather to rise.[221]

[219] Baines, *Cotton Manufacture*, 1835, p. 395.

[220] The figures for calico are taken from Baines, *History of the Cotton Manufacture*, 1835, p. 356; for raw cotton, from Ellison, *Cotton Trade*, 1886, Appendix, Table I.

[221] *Vide* the table given on page 168.

It seems very probable that this increased production led to competition between the various manufacturers which might well be called "cutthroat competition." The domestic market could not absorb all the output, and it was not to the interest of the producers to spoil the domestic market if it could be avoided. Therefore the most bitter phases of this competition were fought out in the foreign markets, and particularly in the American market.

Had the merchant tried to purchase the output of the manufacturer, or even a large part of what he might believe would normally be required for the American market, he would have run the risk—or perhaps faced the certainty—of finding himself in competition with the manufacturers. A merchant who buys outright must be fairly confident of a limited supply, or must buy on the basis of definite contracts. In this period no such condition was possible, for the supply was indeterminate. The manufacturers produced apparently as much as possible, sold what they could to the domestic trade, and consigned the rest to the foreign markets to be sold for what it would bring. Doubtless they expected to cover at least their costs, or if they did not, hoped that the higher price in Great Britain would compensate them; but, if neither of these wishes was fulfilled, realised that they had to keep on as they were or go out of business, for a reduction in the total volume of output might so raise the unit cost of production as to make it difficult or impossible for them to continue to manufacture for the home trade at a profit. The merchant—British or American—could not possibly hope to compete in a market where the prices might at any moment be slashed by a consignment from some desperate manufacturer.

This general line of argument leads to the conclusion that the prices of the same goods was higher in England than it was in America. Theoretically this was possible, for a limited period at least, even although the cost of transportation was added to the cost of the goods. The general theory that the price of a good tends to be the same in all markets, making allowances for differences in costs of transportation, and the custom duties, holds good only when communication is rapid and sure. When, however, it was as slow as it was at the time of which we are speaking, it would have taken a considerable difference in price between America and Great Britain to have tempted a merchant to reëxport goods to the place of origin. Practically, we have no proof of this proposition, although it may be said that it was the belief of the American merchant that goods could be purchased more cheaply in America at times than he could purchase them in Great Britain.[222]

This situation was by no means unnoticed at the time. A witness before the committee of 1833 gave as his reason for the prevailing practice of shipping goods on consignment, or on speculation, the following:

"The manufacturers in England are obliged to operate on a very large scale; they have a regular demand for two-thirds or three-fourths of what they make, and the rest they ship; and their reason for shipping is, that they do not choose to depreciate their own article, and they do not choose to compete with their customers; they can only sell at a fit price a certain quantity, and the excess they export."[223]

In answer to an inquiry as to whether the consignment trade was the result of a "deficiency of ample market at home," he showed that by operating on a large scale and selling the surplus abroad, the manufacturer really gained even though the price in the foreign market was lower than in the domestic market.

"Do you think that the increase of consignments is a proof of deficiency of ample market at home, inasmuch as if the manufacturers had got an abundant market at home, with orders coming to them, they would probably not incur the risk of sending goods abroad?"

"What I understand to be the case is this; suppose that a manufacturer makes 100,000 pieces of calicoes, he has only a regular demand for 75,000, but he finds that with little additional expense, he makes the other 25,000; that arises from the scale upon which he operates. I can state a case that has come under my own observation, which will furnish an illustration of the economy arising from an extended scale of operation. I remember a person in London, a few years ago who was in the iron business; he wanted money; his friends advanced him 20,-000£; he found that, operating with the 20,000£ he could make six per cent; but he showed clearly that if his means were doubled, if he had 40,000£ instead of 20,000£ he could introduce such savings into his business as would yield him a profit of nine per cent, and it is these savings which induce the cotton manufacturer to operate upon the large scale that he does, and which is the cause of this excess. It is not a sacrifice that he makes, because if he sells these goods at an ap-

---

[222] Compare, however, the account on page 138 of the return of the *Electra* to England, laden with goods which could not be sold in America.

[223] Parl. Papers, Report on Manufactures, 1833, p. 93.

parent loss as compared with the goods he sells to his customers, still the general result is profitable to him on account of the saving to which I have alluded."[224]

The merchant of Great Britain did not lose his position of importance by this change in the method of conducting the export trade. While at first many of the manufacturers dealt with their own agents—and many of them continued to do so—a great number of them, as we have seen, chose to make use of the facilities which the merchant had to offer them, in his capacity of commission merchant. An increasing quantity of goods was shipped through the merchant to the American market, although the risk was still placed on the manufacturers. This enabled the shipments to be made more economically in many ways, but it was more important in that it gave to the manufacturer assistance in the conduct of his plant. The universal custom of drawing on the merchant after consignment had been made to him placed at the disposal of the manufacturer the capital resources of the mercantile class, and so promoted continuity of operation, and concentration of effort on the part of the class which was best fitted for manufacturing. The manufacturer was required to spend no part of his time in the actual details of shipment or sale; his attention could be devoted solely to manufacturing. Had he insisted on merchandising as well, as some did, he probably could not have operated on so large a scale and still have operated continuously. The advances made by the mercantile class in this period and later on seem to us to be as significant in the promotion and extension of large-scale industry as the transfer of capital from the mercantile pursuits to manufacturing was in the establishments of the factory system.

We have attempted in the discussion above to explain the predominance of the merchant in the period from 1800-1815, and of the manufacturer, or of the commission merchant, acting as the agent of the manufacturer, in the period from 1815-1830. In conclusion it is necessary briefly to touch upon the position of the American merchant in the Anglo-American trade—more precisely, to try to explain why the American merchant was of less significance than the British merchant, and why he became a more important factor in the trade organisation after 1830.

The answer to this question seems to the writer to lie in the

[224] Parl. Papers, Report on Manufactures, 1833, p. 93.

relation of the capital resources of Great Britain and the United States which were available for the purposes of trade. In general it may be stated that that country which has the greater capital resources will assume the initiative in exporting and in importing; she will be able to purchase her imports on a cash basis, or on very short credit terms, and to sell her own goods on long credit terms. If we examine the trade organisation of Great Britain and the United States today, we find that the exporters and importers meet on a plane of practical equality; on the other hand, in the trade between Great Britain and Latin America, it is the more highly developed and richer country which is in virtual control of the situation.

The ability of the merchants of any country to import on their own account and at their own risk is determined by the terms on which they can sell the goods to their customers. To quote the lowest price possible, they must be able to pay as promptly as the merchants of the nation with which they are in competition. They must be able to meet the credit terms offered by their competitors, selling through their own branch houses or through commission merchants, if they are to retain their customers.

We know that the American jobbers and wholesalers demanded long credit terms, and that they were forced to sell on still longer credit terms to their Western and Southern buyers; the nature of the occupation of the majority of the American people made the extension of credit a necessary feature of business practice. To pay the British manufacturer for goods promptly, and at the same time to extend credit for many months to American buyers was beyond the power of many of the American merchants. The British merchant, with his greater resources, and with the possibility of securing additional financial backing from the London market, was in a position to offer very severe competition for the trade of the American wholesalers and jobbers. Considering the constantly growing demands for capital for the development of the country, and the inadequate supply of American capital, it is rather surprising that, in the period before 1815, there were as many American merchants who can correctly be considered importers as there seem to have been.

The decline in the importance of the American merchant after 1815 was but a natural consequence of the changes in the methods of production in Great Britain, and of the development of the consignment system and sale at auction. In Great Britain a similar change seems to have taken place. So long as forced sales were inevitable no merchant, American or British, could safely venture to handle manufactured goods in large quantities.

The increase in the number of American importing merchants in the period after 1830 can be explained only on very general grounds. We have seen that in this period they bought their goods usually at four months' credit. This indicates an increase in the resources of the mercantile class—for we know that the wholesalers and jobbers to whom they sold did not pay them in so short a period—and suggests refinements in the banking facilities of America, and the enlargement of the resources of the banks, which enabled them to finance the American merchant, if he were unable to do so himself.

It must be borne in mind, however, that the change in the relative position of the American and the British merchant was not of great consequence at the time. A great volume of consignments by British commission merchants and manufacturers continued to flow in. The accumulations of capital in America were not so great as to make the assistance of the British capitalist unnecessary, nor had the demand for permanent investment slackened. It is but the beginning of the gradual assertion of financial independence which we see, the first steps towards meeting the British exporter on terms of equality.

BIBLIOGRAPHICAL NOTE

The securing of material on the subjects treated in this dissertation has been a problem of great difficulty. The way in which the foreign or the domestic trade was carried on in earlier days seems to have been a matter of comparatively little interest to contemporary writers, and it is rare indeed to find any pamphlet or article directly devoted to the subject of trade organisation. A peculiar set of circumstances was necessary to induce a writer to discuss questions of trade organisation, and when he did do so, the discussion was usually incidental to the development of another theme.

It is believed that relatively little assistance can be obtained from contemporary pamphlets and other writings. The writer has had the advantage of access to the Wagner Collection of Economic and Political Tracts deposited in the Yale University Library, and has investigated all the pamphlets or books which seemed at all likely to be of value in this study. While some have proved of great importance, the small number of the contemporary works noted in the bibliography testifies to the lack of weight attached to this phase of foreign trade by the writers of the period.

The most important source of material bearing on the subject of Anglo-American trade organisation has been found to be the reports of various Committees of the Parliament of Great Britain. Although in practically all cases the object of the investigation was not the method of carrying on foreign trade, yet, in the endeavor to elicit testimony on the major question, exceedingly valuable information on the organisation of foreign trade was brought out. The reports themselves are of relatively little value, but the evidence of the merchants, manufacturers, and others who testified before these committees contains statements of the greatest worth, because they represent first-hand knowledge, and because, having been given under oath, they can be deemed trustworthy.

A source of much information on trade organisation should

be found in the business records of firms or individuals actually engaged in foreign trade. The account books, memorandum books, and particularly the letter books, giving the copies of letters written by the firm to its foreign correspondents, would well repay intensive study. The writer has had access to very few records of this nature, and, with the exception of the letter books of William Bostwick, has found none of direct value in this study. The search for business records has been limited, however, to the libraries of Yale and Harvard Universities, the Boston Public Library, and the collections of the Massachusetts Historical Society, where the tendency seems to have been to specialise on the Colonial period, to the neglect of the later period.

Another method of approach which we believe would yield results of great significance is through a study of suits at law involving disputes over shipments of goods. A limited use has been made of these sources, but to obtain the most complete information, one should have access to the records of the court where the case was originally tried, and where the testimony of the witnesses is preserved *in extenso*. Frequently a case turned on the proof that a certain method was or was not the customary manner of doing business. In the very meagre digests of those cases which were appealed to a higher state court or to a federal court, we have found information of importance, and an indication of the existence of much more valuable material in the full reports of the cases.

The bibliography which follows contains only those titles which have been quoted in the text. The titles are arranged alphabetically, with the exception of the Parliamentary Papers and the publications of the United States Government. All the reports of Parliamentary Committees are grouped under "Parliamentary Papers," according to the date of publication. It was found necessary to abbreviate the titles of these reports when quoting them in the footnotes, and, in order to avoid any confusion, the abbreviated title is given first, and is then followed by the complete title, with the year of publication, the volume, and the serial number of the respective session of Parliament. A similar plan has been followed in the case of the United States government publications: the reports are listed in order of publication under the general heading, "United States Government Publications."

It was not felt desirable to include in the bibliography a list of the reports of legal cases cited in the text. The full reference to each case is given in the footnotes, and the method of citing such cases has been so standardised that the reader should have no difficulty in locating the particular case to which reference is made.

BIBLIOGRAPHY

An Account of the Proceedings of the Merchants, Manufacturers and others concerned in the Wool and Woollen Trade of Great Britain in their Application to Parliament. London, 1800.

The Anglo-French Treaty.

The Cotton Trade of Lancaster and the Anglo-French Commercial Treaty of 1860. A Report of the English Evidence at the French Commercial Inquiry of 1870. Translated by John Slagg, Jr. London (no date).

The Anomalies of the Cotton Trade: the Liverpool brokerage system, by a Cotton Spinner. Manchester, 1841.

BAINES, EDWARD, JR. History of the Cotton Manufacture in Great Britain. London, 1835.

The Bankers' Magazine. Baltimore, 1847-1850. New York, 1853—

The Bankers' Magazine. London, 1844—

BARING, ALEXANDER (Baron Ashburton). An Inquiry into the causes and consequences of the Orders in Council and an Examination of the Conduct of Great Britain toward the Neutral Commerce of America. London, 1808. (New York ed. 1808 quoted.)

BOLLES, A. S. The Financial History of the United States, from 1789 to 1860. New York, 1883. (2d ed. 1885 quoted.)

Boston Almanac and Business Directory. Boston, annual, 1836—

BOSTWICK, WILLIAM. Letter Books, 4 vol., June, 1826, to February, 1848. MSS. deposited in Yale University Library.

BROOKE, RICHARD. Liverpool, at it was. . . . Liverpool, 1853.

CAINES, GEORGE. Lex Mercatoria Americana, 2 vol. New York, 1802.

CALLENDER, GUY S. English Capital and American Resources, 1815-1860. 1897. MSS. deposited in Harvard College Library.

CHAPMAN, SYDNEY J. The Lancashire Cotton Industry. Manchester, 1904.

CHITTY, JOSEPH. Treatise on Laws of Commerce and Manufactures, 4 vol. London, 1824.

The City; or, The Physiology of London Business; with Sketches on 'Change, and at the Coffee Houses. (David M. Evans.) London, 1845.

CLAPHAM, J. H. The Woollen and Worsted Industries. London, 1907.

CLARKE, VICTOR S. A History of Manufactures, 1607-1860. Washington, 1916.

A Commercial Dictionary. . . . Pub. by J. C. Kayser and Company. Philadelphia, 1823.

Compendium of the Enumeration of the Inhabitants and Statistics of the United States, as obtained at the Department of State from the Returns of the Sixth Census. Washington, 1841.

DANIELS, G. W. American Cotton Trade with Liverpool under the Embargo and Non-Intercourse Acts. *Am. Hist. Rev.*, 1916, vol. XXI, pp. 276-287.

DANIELS, G. W. The Early English Cotton Industry. London, 1920.

DANIELS, G. W. The Early Records of a Great Manchester Cotton-Spinning Firm. *Econ. Journal* (London), 1915, vol. XXV, pp. 175-188.

DeBow's Review, ed. by J. D. B. DeBow. New Orleans, 1846-1862; published under different titles:

The Commercial Review of the South and West, 1846-1850.

DeBow's Review of the Southern and Western States, 1850-1852.

DeBow's Review and Industrial Resources, Statistics, etc., 1853-1862.

DEWEY, DAVID R. Financial History of the United States. New York, 1912, 4th ed.

The Edinburgh Review. Edinburgh, 1803-1890. London, 1890—

EDWARDS, ISAAC. An Essay on Brokers and Factors or Commission Merchants. Albany, 1870.

ELLISON, THOMAS. The Cotton Trade of Great Britain. London, 1886.

Encyclopædia Americana, 13 vol. Philadelphia, 1830.

ENFIELD, WILLIAM. An Essay towards the History of Leverpool. London, 1774, 2d ed.

ENTZ, JOHN F. Exchange and Cotton Trade between England and the United States. Charleston and New York, 1840.

An Essay on the Effects of the Inequitable Modes of Pursuing Trade, with Analogous Remedies: comprising a Dissertation upon the Diminution and Remuneration of Labor. By a Liveryman of London. London, 1813-1814.

Facts, important to be known by the Manufacturers, Mechanics etc. (Selected from a pamphlet, 1828, "Remarks upon the Auction System as practiced in New York . . ."). New York, 1831.

The Federal Union. Milledgeville, Georgia.

The Financial Register of the United States, 2 vol. Pub. by Wirtz and Tatem. Philadelphia, July, 1837, to December, 1838.

FRASER, CHARLES. Reminiscences of Charleston. Charleston, 1854.

FUCHS, C. J. Die Organisation der Liverpooler Baumwollhandels in Vergangenheit und Gegenwart. Jahrbuch für Gesetzgebung (Schmoller), 1890, vol. XIV, p. 107.

HAMMOND, M. B. The Cotton Industry. Am. Econ. Assn. Publ. (new series), No. 1, 1897.

HEATON, HERBERT. The Yorkshire Woollen and Worsted Industries. Oxford, 1920. (Vol. X of the Oxford Historical and Literary Studies.)

Hunt's *Merchants' Magazine and Commercial Review*. New York, 1840-1870.

JAMES, JOHN. History of the Worsted Manufacture in England. London, 1857.

JOPLIN, T. Articles on Banking and Currency, from *The Economist Newspaper*. London, 1838.

LEE, HENRY. Letters to the Cotton Manufacturers of Massachusetts, 2 vol. n.d.n.p. [1843]. (Harvard College Library.)

Letter Book. *Vide* William Bostwick.

LIPSON, E. The History of the Woollen and Worsted Industries. London, 1921.

The Liverpool Mercury. Pub. at Liverpool, England (weekly), 1811—

The London Tradesman. A Familiar Treatise on the Rationale of Trade and Commerce, as carried on in the Metropolis of the British Empire, by several Tradesmen. London, 1819, 2d ed., 1820.

McCULLOCH, J. R. A Dictionary, practical, theoretical, and historical, of Commerce, and Commercial Navigation. London, 1834, 2d ed.

MacGREGOR, JOHN. Commercial Statistics. A digest of the productive resources, commercial legislation, . . . of all Nations, 5 vol. London, 1850, 2d ed.

McMASTER, JOHN B. Life and Times of Stephen Girard, Mariner and Merchant, 2 vol. Philadelphia, 1918.

MacPHERSON, DAVID. Annals of Commerce, Manufactures, Fisheries, and Navigation, 4 vol. London, 1805.

MARSHALL, JOHN. A Digest of the accounts relating to the Population, Production, Revenues . . . of the United Kingdom. London, 1834.

Matters of Fact relative to the Licence-Trade and Foreign Shipping. London, 1812.

Memorial of the Auctioneers of the City of New York. Washington 1821 (37). Printed by order of the Senate.

Memorial of the Chamber of Commerce of the City of New York. Washington, 1820 (32).

Memorial of a Convention of the Friends of National Industry assembled in the City of New York. Washington, 1819 (9).

Memorial of the Merchants of Baltimore, praying that the duties on Imported Merchandise may be paid in Cash. Washington, 1820 (30).

Memorial of the merchants, and others interested in commerce in Salem and its vicinity to the Congress of the United States, on the discontinuance of credits on revenue bonds, the abolition of drawbacks, and other restrictions on Commerce. Salem, 1820.

MONTEFIORE, JOSHUA. A Commercial Dictionary, 1 vol. London, 1803, unpaged. 1st American ed., 3 vol. Philadelphia, 1804.

Niles' *Weekly Register*, 75 vol. Baltimore, 1811-1849.

New Orleans Price Current and *Commercial Intelligencer*. Pub. at New Orleans, Louisiana (weekly) (1823-1883 in Library of Congress).

The North American Review. Boston, 1815-1877. New York, 1878—

PAGE, WILLIAM. Commerce and Industry, Tables of Statistics for the British Empire from 1815, 2 vol. London, 1919.

Parliamentary Papers (Great Britain).

Reports on Linen Trade.

Report from the Select Committee on the Petition of the dealers in, and Manufacturers of Linens, etc. 1744. Reports from Committees, 1st Series, vol. II, p. 65.

Report from the Select Committee appointed to examine the Petitions Respecting the Linen Manufacture. 1751. Reports from Committees, 1st Series, vol. II, p. 287.

Reports on High Price of Provisions.

Seven Reports from the Select Committee to consider the High Price of Provisions. Reports from Committees, 1st Series, vol. IX, and Session 1801, vol. II (174).

Report on Woolen Manufacture.

Report from the Select Committee on the state of the Woollen Manufacture of England. Session 1806, vol. III (268, 268a).

Minutes of Evidence.

Minutes of Evidence . . . upon taking into consideration the Petition of several Merchants of Liverpool; and also, The Petition of several Merchants, Manufacturers, and others of the City of London, interested in the Trade with the United States. . . . Session 1808 (119).

Report on the State of Commercial Credit.

Report from the Select Committee on the State of Commercial Credit. Session 1810-1811, vol. II (52).

Report on Orders in Council.

Minutes of Evidence taken before the Committee of the Whole House, to whom it was referred, to consider of the several PETITIONS which have been presented to the House, in this Session of Parliament, relating to the ORDERS IN COUNCIL. Session 1812 (210).

Report on Corn Laws.

Report from the Select Committee on petitions relating to the Corn Laws of this Kingdom. Session 1813-1814, vol. III (339).

Report on Grain and Corn Law.

Reports from the Lords' Committee on the State of the Growth, Commerce, and Consumption of Grain, and all Laws relating thereto. Session 1814-1815, vol. V (26).

Report on Assize of Bread.

Report from the Select Committee Relating to the Manufacture, Sale, and Assize of Bread. Session 1814-1815, vol. V (186).

Report on Duties on Cotton Prints.

Report from the Select Committee on the Duties payable on Printed Cotton Goods, etc. Session 1818, vol. III (279).

Report on Cash Payments.

Report and Minutes of Evidence of the Secret Committee on the Expediency of the Bank Resuming Cash Payments. Session 1819, vol. III (202, 282).

Reports on Foreign Trade.

Report from the Select Committee on Improving the Foreign Trade of the Country. Session 1820, vol. II (300).

First Report from the Select Committee of the House of Lords, appointed to inquire into the means of extending and securing the Foreign Trade of the Country [relative to the timber trade]. Session 1820, vol. III (269).

Report from the Select Committee of the House of Lords, appointed to inquire into the means of extending and securing the Foreign Trade of the Country [relative to the trade with the East Indies and China]. Session 1821, vol. VII (476).

Second Report from the Select Committee of the House of Lords, appointed . . . [relative to the silk and wine trade]. Session 1821, vol. VII (703).

First Report from the Select Committee appointed to consider the Means of improving and maintaining the Foreign Trade of the Country [relative to the timber trade]. Session 1821, vol. VI (186).

Third Report from the Select Committee appointed to consider . . . the Foreign Trade of the Country [relative to the trade with the East Indies and China]. Session 1821, vol. VI (746).

Report on the State of Agriculture.

Report from the Select Committee on Petitions complaining of the depressed state of Agriculture of the United Kingdom. Session 1821, vol. IX (668).

Report on Linen Trade.

Report from the Select Committee on the Laws which regulate the Linen Trade of Ireland. Session 1822, vol. VII (560).

Report on Merchants.

Report from the Select Committee on the Law relating to Merchants, Agents, or Factors. Session 1823, vol. IV (452).

Report on the Price of Foreign Grain.

Report from the Select Committee of the House of Lords . . . [on] the Price [of] Shipping Foreign Grain from Foreign Ports. Session 1826-1827, vol. VI (333).

Report on British Wool Trade.

Report from the Select Committee of the House of Lords on the state of the British Wool Trade. Session 1828, vol. VIII (515).

Accounts and Papers. Session 1830-1831, vol. X (145).

Official value of the Cotton Manufactures . . .

Report on Bank of England Charter.
  Report from the Committee of Secrecy on the expediency of re-
  newing the Charter of the Bank of England, and on the system
  on which the Banks of Issue in England and Wales are conducted.
  Session 1831-1832, vol. VI (722).
Report on Manufactures.
  Report from the Select Committee on the present state of Manu-
  factures, Commerce, and Shipping in the United Kingdom. Ses-
  sion 1833, vol. VI (690).
Report on Hand-Loom Weavers.
  Report from the Select Committee on Petitions from the Hand-
  Loom Weavers. Session 1834, vol. X (556).
Report on Condition of Frame Work Knitters.
  Report on the Commissioner appointed to Inquire into the Con-
  ditions of the Frame Work Knitters. Presented to both Houses of
  Parliament by Command of her Majesty. Session 1845, vol. XXIII.
  (Appendix, vol. XXIV.)
Report of the Inspector of Factories.
  For quarter ending 30th September, 1844; and from 1st October,
  1844, to 30th April, 1845. Session 1845, vol. XXV.
Reports on Commercial Distress.
  First and Second Reports from the Secret Committee of the House
  of Commons on Commercial Distress. Session 1847-1848, vol.
  XXVII (1st report, 213; 2d report, 213-II); vol. XXVIII. (Ap-
  pendix, 213-III.)
  Report from the Secret Committee of the House of Lords ap-
  pointed to inquire into the Causes of the Distress which has for
  some time prevailed among the Commercial Classes, and how far
  it has been affected by the Laws for regulating the Issue of Bank
  Notes payable on Demand, together with minutes of Evidence, and
  an Appendix. Session 1847-1848, vol. XXIV (31).
PITKIN, TIMOTHY. Statistical View of the Commerce of the United
  States. Hartford, 1816.
PORTER, G. R. The Progress of the Nation. London, 1836. (Revised
  edition by F. W. Hirst, London, 1912, quoted.)
Preston. The Commercial Directory of Preston and its Environs. . . .
  A complete classification is given of the names, designation and ad-
  dress of the Merchants—Professional Gentlemen—Manufacturers
  and Tradesmen generally. Published by P. and H. Whittle, Preston,
  Eng., 1842.
Report on the Committee of Investigation, appointed at the Meeting
  of the Stockholders of the Bank of the United States, Held January
  4, 1841. Philadelphia, 1841.
Report of the Lords of the Committee of Council. Dublin, 1795.
SALOMONS, DAVID. The Monetary Difficulties of America and their
  Probable Effects on British Commerce considered. London, 1837.

SCHULZE-GAEVERNITZ, GUSTAVE VON. Der Grossbetrieb ein wirtschaft-
licher und socialer Fortschritt. Eine studie auf dem Gebiete der
Baumwoll Industrie. Leipzig, 1892. Translated by O. S. Hall as
"Cotton Trade in England and on the Continent," London, 1895.
English translation quoted.

SEABROOK, WHITMARSH B. A Memoir on the Origin, Uses and Cultivation of Cotton. Charleston, 1844.

SEYBERT, ADAM. Statistical Annals. Philadelphia, 1818.

SHAW, J. T. The Wool Trade of the United States; its Rise and Progress in Boston. Boston, 1909. (Republished as Sen. Doc. no. 70, 61st
Cong., 1st Sess., 1909.)

SLACK, JOHN. Commercial Caution; an exposition of the Nature of
Trade and . . . Remarks on Cotton. Manchester, 1835.

SMITHERS, HENRY. Liverpool, its Commerce, Statistics, and Institu-
tions, with a History of the Cotton Trade. Liverpool, 1825.

The South in the Building of the Nation, 12 vol. Richmond, 1909.
(Volume V contains a series of articles on the economic history of
the South.)

The Southern Trade, An Epitome of Commerce, North and South.
Semiannual, 1859———. Pub. by E. K. Cooley, New York.

STONE, A. H. Cotton Factorage System of the Southern States. Am.
Hist. Rev., 1915, vol. XX, pp. 557-565.

TALLEYRAND, LE CITOYEN. Mémoire sur les Relations Commerciales des
Etats-Unis avec l'Angleterre. London, 1805.

TATE, W. The Elements of Commercial Calculations and an Introduction to the Most Important Branches of the Commerce and Finance
of this Country, 2 vol. London, 1819.

TOMKINS, DANIEL A. Money in Cotton Growing. Published in Southern
States, July, 1897.

Trade and Commerce of New York from 1815 to the present time, A
Review of the. By an observer. New York, 1820.

TROTTER, ALEXANDER. Observations of the Financial Position and
Credit of such of the States of the North American Union as have
contracted Public Debts. London, 1839.

United States Government Publications.

Report on Cash Duties and the Warehouse System. Committee on
Commerce. H. R. 93, 20th Cong., 3d Sess., Feb., 1829.

A Report on the Cultivation, Manufacture, and Foreign Trade of
Cotton. Levi Woodbury, Secretary of the Treasury. House Execu-
tive Doc. 146, 24th Cong., 1st Sess., 1836.

Report on the Warehouse System. Committee on Ways and Means.
H. R. 195, 24th Cong., 2d Sess., Feb., 1837.

Report on the Warehouse System. Committee on Commerce (Mr.
Kennedy). H. R. 103, 27th Cong., 3d Sess., 1843.

Report of the Committee on Manufactures, H. R. no. 67, 40th Cong.,
2d Sess., June, 1868.

Report of the Special Commissioner of Revenue (David A. Wells). House Ex. Doc. 16, 40th Cong., 3d Sess., 1869.

Statistical Tables Exhibiting the Commerce of the United States with European Countries, from 1790 to 1890. Bureau of Statistics, Treasury Department. House Mis. Doc. 117, 52d Cong., 2d Sess., 1893.

WESTERFIELD, RAY B. Early History of American Auctions—a Chapter in Commercial History. Trans. of the Conn. Academy of Arts and Sciences. New Haven, May, 1920, vol. XXIII, pp. 159-210.

WESTERFIELD, RAY B. Middlemen in English Business, Particularly Between 1660 and 1760. Trans. of the Conn. Academy of Arts and Sciences. New Haven, May, 1915, vol. XIX, pp. 111-445.

WHITTLE, P. A topographical, statistical and historical Account of the Borough of Preston. Preston, vol. I, 1821 (contains directory for 1821); vol. 2, 1837.

INDEX